Via Be

Crittenden Marriott

Alpha Editions

This edition published in 2024

ISBN : 9789362926289

Design and Setting By
Alpha Editions
www.alphaedis.com
Email - info@alphaedis.com

Contents

PREFACE

The veil of diplomacy screens many secrets—most of them for many years. But the veil is not impenetrable; from time to time a corner lifts, disclosing a fact long-suspected but never quite comprehended, a fact that fits into a history thitherto incomplete.

So of this tale! Its substance is not altogether new. For years rumors of it have floated in and out of diplomatic antechambers in half truths and partial explanations that lacked the master key that would give them form and coherence. Now, now when the event itself is well-nigh forgotten, comes the great war to supply the key to the puzzle—the missing fragment, round which all the other fragments range themselves in one consistent whole.

Fancy? Guesswork? Gossip? Perhaps. The veil has dropped again and much may still be hidden behind it. But those who read the tale in the light of later events—of events of yesterday and events still in progress—are likely to put more faith in it than in many of the solemn lies of history.

CHAPTER I

The Secretary of State leaned back in his chair and studied the young man before him. "Sit down, Mr. Topham," he said at last.

Topham sat down. He was a good-looking young fellow, soldierly and straight as a ramrod, but without the stiffness that usually goes with a military carriage. His tanned face and, in fact, his whole bearing spoke of an out-door life—probably a life on the sea. Such an occupation was also indicated by his taciturnity, for he said nothing, though the secretary waited long, as if to give him a chance to speak.

Finally the secretary seemed satisfied. "Mr. Topham," he said, "I have asked you to call on me for a purpose not connected, so far as I see at present, with your mission to Japan. Concerning that, I have nothing to add to the instructions already given you. Your reports will, of course, be to the Secretary of the Navy and you will of course not forget that your duties as naval attaché to our embassy at Tokio include the sending of any political information you may be able to pick up, in addition to such naval and military details as you may consider of importance. You speak Japanese, I believe?"

Topham bowed. "A little," he replied, modestly.

"More than a little, I understand," corrected the Secretary. "Doubtless you will find your knowledge of great advantage to you in your work. It is not of this, however, but of something quite different that I wish to speak."

The Secretary paused, as if to give the young man a chance, but the latter said nothing. He merely waited courteously until the Secretary resumed.

"Have you any special preference as to your route to Japan?" he asked.

Topham shook his head. "Very little," he answered. "I have scarcely had time. I supposed vaguely that I should go by San Francisco, because that was the most direct route, but it makes no difference to me."

"I should like you to go by Europe and the Suez Canal. Have you any personal reason for desiring to go by Berlin?"

"Berlin? I don't know! Er—Isn't Mr. Rutile secretary of embassy there?"

The secretary's eyebrows went up a trifle. "Yes!" he answered. To Topham his voice sounded a little sharp.

"He was at Annapolis with me, but resigned shortly after being graduated. We were always chums and I should be very glad to see him again."

"Very well! That will serve as an excellent excuse for your choice of route. Kindly indicate to Admiral Brownson of the Bureau of Navigation your desire to proceed by way of Berlin, and he will issue the necessary orders. You will find that these will direct you to proceed with due diligence via Berlin to Brindisi, where you will join the U. S. S. Nevada as watch officer, relieving Lieutenant Shoreham, who is to be invalided home. You will proceed on the Nevada to Manila, where you will be detached, and will proceed at once to Tokio."

The Secretary paused and picked a long official document before him. "You might mention your plans to any officer or others whom you chance to meet. I wish your choice of route to appear as natural as possible. You understand?"

Topham bowed. "I understand, sir," he replied.

"Very good. Now, Mr. Topham, permit me to ask whether your mention of Mr. Rutile just now was purely accidental or whether you had any information that I wanted you to take a confidential message to him."

Topham laughed. "Do you really?" he asked. "No! Mr. Secretary! I had no idea or information to that effect. It was altogether a coincidence, I assure you."

"Ah! I was beginning to wonder if there was a leak in my office. Well! Mr. Topham, I wish you would take this packet and deliver it with your own hands in private to Mr. Rutile. You must not let even the ambassador know that you are carrying documents of any kind. No one is to know, except Mr. Rutile and yourself. You understand?"

"Surely, sir."

"Very good. Can you leave for New York tonight?"

"Certainly, sir."

"Please do so! I am sorry to curtail your stay in Washington, but there is no time to lose. Your passage has been taken on the steamer Marlatic, which leaves for Hamburg tomorrow morning. Make all the speed you can to Brindisi, remembering, however, that it is better to lose a day or two than by any undue haste to cast doubt on the credibility of your visit to Berlin. The Nevada will wait for you, though she is badly needed at Manila."

"I understand, sir!"

The secretary cleared his throat. "You will understand, Mr. Topham," he went on, "that I do not make a messenger out of you without good cause. It is very important that these documents should reach Mr. Rutile promptly and secretly. Probably you will make the trip without the least misadventure. Remember, however, that there are people who would be exceedingly anxious to get a look at these papers if they should learn of their existence. I cannot warn you of them specifically, because I do not know who they are. We have tried to keep secret the fact that any papers are being sent, and this is one reason for choosing you. I think we have succeeded, but one can never tell. If the fact has gotten out attempts may be made to take the papers from you either by fraud or violence. I do not know how far the people who want them would go in their efforts to rob you, but it is quite possible that they might go to the limit. Be warned, therefore, and be prepared to frustrate any attempt of any sort whatever. You understand, Mr. Topham?"

Topham stood up. "I think so, sir," he replied.

"Very good. Here is the packet." The Secretary passed it over. "That is all, Mr. Topham. Good luck." He rose, and held out his hand.

Topham bowed and took his departure. Obedient to the secretary's instructions he went along the corridor to the offices of the Bureau of Navigation of the Navy Department, and explained to the admiral in charge his desire to go via Berlin. Evidently the affair was cut and dried, for his orders were made out and placed in his hands in an amazingly few minutes.

While he waited for them he mentioned to several navy friends the route that he would take and his reasons for desiring it, and made inquiries concerning the officer whom he was to relieve. Later, when, orders in hand, he made his way to the entrance of the building he met an old newspaper friend, to whom he casually mentioned his prospective journey.

Under the big portico he stopped and drew a long breath. Events had moved so fast in the last few hours that he was almost bewildered. He had only reached Washington about noon on that same day, having been detached from his ship at Hampton Roads. On his arrival, he had been questioned concerning his reported acquaintance with the Japanese language, and had been notified to prepare to leave at once for Tokio as naval attaché to the embassy there. He had received detailed instructions, both written and oral, as to the duties of his post; and then had been sent to the Secretary of State for further confidential instructions which had taken the shape described.

His watch showed that barely five hours had elapsed since he had entered the building, with no thought either of Japan or Berlin in his mind. And now he was practically en route for both. The rapidity of the thing made his head swim. "Almost like war times," he muttered. "Great Scott! I wonder if we really are going to have trouble with the Japs!"

With a shrug of his shoulders he dismissed the matter from his mind. It was no business of his for the moment at least. Again he looked at his watch. "Half-past five o'clock," he muttered, hesitating.

He need not leave for New York before midnight, and the temptation was strong upon him to spend a few hours in looking up the friends he had made during his tour of duty at the Capital City two years before. They were very good friends, many of them, and he would enjoy meeting them.

Only one thing made him pause and that was the thought of Lillian Byrd— if she still were Lillian Byrd. She had played with him, laughed at him, and tossed him over for a wealthier man. When she did so, he had asked for sea duty and had gotten it. He believed that the two years he had spent afloat had healed the wound, and yet he hesitated to risk testing it. Everything and every one he would see would remind him of the days when he lived in a fool's paradise. Why should he torture himself with the vain recollection. He would not! He would take the next train for New York and leave Washington with its friends, foes, and sweethearts behind him.

An hour later he was speeding northward.

CHAPTER II

Topham was on board the Marlatic in good time the next morning.

He found himself in the midst of a jolly laughing throng that crowded and pushed and hugged and kissed and wept a little sometimes, but that the most part gave itself up to a perpetual chattering, like a flock of magpies—with more noise but with little more sense. All sorts of people were there, from the brandnew bride on her honeymoon to the gray old lady who was taking her granddaughter abroad; from the Cook's tourist to the blasé young man who talked airily about crossing the "pond" and the grumpy globe trotter who hated the noise and confusion with his whole heart.

Topham leaned on the rail of the hurricane deck and watched the crowd idly. Somehow he felt lonely. Everybody else had friends; he seemed alone in having no one to see him off. It struck him suddenly that his life was a very lonely one. If Lillian Byrd had not proved faithless—

His ranging eyes fell upon a girl who was just coming up the plank in the wake of a granite-faced chaperone, and the current of his thoughts snapped short off. She was young, scarcely more than twenty, he judged, but there was something about her—he scarcely knew what—that set his pulses to pounding. With his whole strength he stared, and, as though drawn by his glance, the girl suddenly lifted her face and looked directly at him.

For an instant his heart stood still, then raced as it had never raced before, not even when Lillian Byrd had smiled at him in days gone by.

Never had he seen such eyes. They held him, enthralled him, with a magic that went beyond any reasoned process of the human brain. They seemed to fill the girl's whole face—to fill it so that Topham thought he did not notice its other features; though later, he found that he could picture its every detail—the great masses of red-black hair; the clear dusky skin with a rose hiding in each cheek; the nose, chin, and teeth in keeping—not regular, not perfect according to canons of art, but compelling; a face for which men die.

Recklessly the navy officer stared—stared till the red flamed in the girl's cheek, and she stumbled, her trembling fingers loosing their hold upon the rail.

She must have said something, though Topham could not hear her, for the hard-faced chaperone turned and caught her arm. Topham saw her shake her head in negation to some question. The next instant she looked up once more. But not as before! Coldly her glance swept Topham's face, as coldly as if he did not exist. Then, before he could even attempt to catch her eyes, she had stepped upon the deck and was hidden from his view.

Topham drew his breath gaspingly. He had been holding it for quite a minute, unknowingly. His thoughts ran riot. Who was she? Who was she? What was her race, her state, her name? Her face bespoke a southern parentage; the blood that burned beneath it cried aloud of tropic heat. But her blue eyes were of the north. And the chaperone by her side could be nothing else than German—a veritable grenadier.

Certainly they were people of distinction in their own land—probably in any land. The purser might know. He would go and ask.

The purser was affable but tremendously busy. Yes, he knew the lady. She had crossed on the Marlatic a few weeks before. She was a Senorita Elsa Ferreira, a Brazilian lady who was connected with a famous German family. The lady with her was the Baroness Ostersacken. If Mr. Topham wanted any more information, he would endeavor to oblige him later on. At the present moment, however, in the hurry of departure, he—

Topham thanked him and went on deck, feeling the throb of the propeller beneath his feet as he did so. The steamer was in midstream heading toward the lower bay and the open sea.

For an hour or more Topham paced the deck hoping in vain for another sight of the girl who had so fascinated him. The wind was blowing strongly, and as the Marlatic approached Sandy Hook, she began to pitch with, the motion of the Atlantic rollers, and her passengers began to disappear. When she crossed the bar all but a handful had deserted the decks. Many seats were vacant when the gong rang for luncheon, and as Miss Ferreira did not appear, Topham began to fear that she was a poor sailor who would keep her cabin all throughout the voyage.

All afternoon he paced the deck despite the increasing unpleasantness of the weather. Darkness fell early and when he came up from dinner and from a tour of the main saloon without seeing anything of the girl, he was forced to abandon hope of finding her that night.

As he leaned grumpily over the rail watching the dim white caps that chased each other athwart the course of the ship, one of the few passengers on deck came and leaned by his side.

"It makes rough, eh! senor?" said the man. "We shall have storm? What you think?"

At the soft Spanish accent, Topham looked quickly up and recognized a Spanish-looking personage whom he remembered having seen crossing the gang plank.

"Oh! no!" he replied, lightly. "I think not. It's damp and cold and unpleasant, but not stormy. Tomorrow will probably be clear."

"That is good. I no like the storm. It is bad for the—the stomach, do you say, senor? I no get sick, but I feel sorry for the others." He took out a package of cigarettes and offered them to Topham. "You smoke, senor?" he asked.

Cigarettes were not Topham's failing, but he helped himself nevertheless. He was lonely and wanted companionship. Besides, the man seemed to be a Spanish-American and anything from Spanish-America had a special charm for Topham since he had heard that Miss Ferreira was from that part of the world.

For a few moments the two men puffed in silence, chatting of indifferent subjects. Then the ship pitched more heavily than usual and the other gulped.

"I—I no get sick," he protested. "I am old sailor. But I—I think I eat something for dinner that not agree with me. I—I think I go below." He slouched heavily away.

Topham did not laugh. With astonishment he had suddenly discovered that he too was feeling qualmy. The sensation was so novel, so utterly unlooked for, so hatefully amazing that he almost laughed.

"By Jove!" he exclaimed. "I'm feeling queer myself. I didn't know that any sea could make me sick, but—Good Lord!"

The sensations had grown stronger with unexampled rapidity. In almost a moment they became acute. A fog came before his eyes and his senses actually reeled. Desperately he clung to the rail, feeling certain that he should fall if his grip loosened.

How long he stood there more than half unconscious he never knew. He was roused by a woman's voice, speaking excitedly.

"But he is ill! He is very ill! Quick! catch him!"

Dimly he heard a faint rush of feet; then an arm was slipped under his. "This way, senor," pleaded a voice—a very soft, musical voice. "Just a step—just a step. Now sit down! There!"

Guided by some one's arm Topham reeled for an immeasurable distance. Then he fell also immeasurably. Finally, finding himself in a chair he closed his eyes.

Only a few seconds later, it seemed, he opened them again and found himself stretched in a steamer chair. His head felt queer and his stomach shaky. As he gazed stupidly around, a woman who was bending over him straightened up.

"It's all right!" said the voice. "He's coming to."

Instinctively Topham struggled to his feet despite the girl's protests. He could see little more than her figure in the semi-darkness, but he nevertheless felt sure that it was she. "Miss Ferreira!" he murmured.

"Oh! you are better! senor! I am glad." Her English was perfect except for a soft Castilian burr.

Topham strove to answer, and succeeded better than he hoped. "Yes! I'm better. Thanks to you! senorita. Heavens, I don't know what got into me! I haven't been seasick since—since—. Is this your chair?"

"Yes! But do not leave it, I beg. I had just come on deck when I noticed that you were ill. Perhaps you ate something for dinner that disagreed with you."

"Perhaps!" ruefully. "That's the usual excuse for getting seasick, you know. However—Good Heavens!"

Topham's heart almost stopped beating. He whipped his hand into his inner coat pocket and found—nothing! Desperately he snatched at another pocket—and another!

With distended eyes the girl stared at him. "You have lost something, senor?" she queried.

"Lost! Lost! Good Heavens, I—" Suddenly Topham dropped his hands and laughed aloud. "Oh! What an idiot I am!" he cried. "No! I haven't lost anything, senorita. I must be daffy. I was looking for something, forgetting that I had put it away for safe-keeping."

CHAPTER III

Topham woke the next day with a splitting headache and a slight but persistent nausea—about what might have been expected after his experience of the night before. The sea had gone down considerably and though the steamer still rolled somewhat, it no longer pitched to any degree that should have been in the least disquieting to an at all seasoned stomach. So Topham rolled out of bed and got on deck as soon as possible. The fresh air slowly restored him to his normal condition and by noon little remained to remind him of his humiliating experience.

He saw nothing of Senorita Ferreira, and though he kept a continual hopeful watch for her, he yet did not altogether regret her absence as it gave him a chance to think things out.

All the forenoon he lay in his steamer chair drinking in the sea-air and pondering the situation. In some points his illness had been unlike any seasickness he had ever heard of; though not entirely dissimilar to some cases of which he had heard. He felt certain that it was not an entirely natural illness, but was very uncertain whether it had resulted from an accidental bane in something he had eaten or whether he had been deliberately drugged. If he had been drugged, it could have been done with no other purpose than to rob him of the packet confided to him by the Secretary of State. He blessed the forethought that had led him to get the purser to lock it up in the ship's safe. Struck by a sudden idea he went below and examined his baggage, but could discover no sign that it had been searched.

The incident, whether resulting from accident or design, brought home to him the seriousness of his errand. If he had really been the victim of a deliberate attempt at robbery, it proved that the cause of his journey to Berlin was no secret and that daring and unscrupulous foes were watching him. He had fooled them once, but the voyage was scarcely begun, and it was not conceivable that they would not follow up the attack. Topham was as brave as most men, but he felt himself at a serious disadvantage; his enemies knew him—probably knew all about him—and he knew nothing of them, neither their age nor their sex nor their number.

It behooved him to find them out if possible. Naturally his first thought was of the soft-spoken Spanish-American who had offered him a cigarette. What was in that cigarette, he wondered. Was anything in it? Had he really been unconscious and if so, for how long? Had he been practically so while he stood clutching the rail or had he only become so after he had been helped to the chair by Senorita Ferreira? Was she in the plot—if there was a plot?

He could contemplate this last possibility calmly, for it never occurred to him to impute moral turpitude to those whose interests ran counter to his in a game of high politics such as this seemed to be.

Think as he might, however, he could not answer any of the questions that were puzzling him. All he could do was for the situation to develop itself. He would speak to the Spaniard, but he knew that he could hope to gain little by doing so. That gentleman, he was sure, would be provided with an unimpeachable defense.

As for Senorita Ferreira—Well! he had no real reason to suspect her—or anyone else, for that matter. Probably, indeed, she had come up in time to frighten off his real assailant.

"All's well that ends well," he decided, finally. "If my Dago friend really did drug me to get the packet, he got decidedly left. On the other hand, I've got an opening with the girl. I'll take her innocence for granted till I see mighty good reason to do otherwise. I wonder where she is, by the way?"

It was not till afternoon, however that the girl came on deck.

She was alone and Topham went straight to her side. "Pardon me," he said. "I want to thank you for your great kindness last night."

The girl smiled at him. "I hope you feel better, senor!" she said.

"Much better! Seasickness is humiliating, but it isn't lasting. I am all right, except that I am still a little shaky on my legs." As he spoke Topham wobbled with what he hoped was artistic verisimilitude.

The girl uttered a little cry. "Oh!" she exclaimed. "You must not stand. Take this chair." She indicated the one next to hers and Topham sank into it with a sigh of content.

Two hours later when the dinner gong sounded, the girl started and looked at her watch. "Good gracious!" she exclaimed. "How the day has gone. I make you my compliments, senor! You have made the time fly."

She rose and Topham regretfully followed suit.

"I hope you will give me another opportunity, senorita," he pleaded.

"But yes. Most certainly! I shall be charmed." With a smile and a nod she was gone.

The most of the voyage—or as much of it as the proprieties and the Baroness Ostersacken would permit—Topham spent by Miss Ferreira's side. Day after day the two watched the shadows shorten, vanish, and grow long once more. Night after night they saw the moon sail across the star-dusted sky, and watched the ripples break athwart her silvery reflection in the water. Day after day, night after night they grew into each other's thoughts—while the Baroness Ostersacken played propriety in the background.

By the end of the voyage each had learned much about the other. Topham had learned that the girl was the daughter of a German mother and a Brazilian father and that she was returning from a trip to Rio Janiero, made in charge of her cousin the Baroness, to join her brother at Berlin. She, on the other hand, learned that Topham was a navy officer, en route for Tokio, who was going via Berlin to see an old friend, and would thence go to Brindisi to join his ship. Not a word nor a suggestion from either had reference to any papers he might carry.

Long before the end of the voyage Topham had made up his mind that this was the one girl in the world for him. His earlier affection for Lillian Byrd he had absolutely forgotten or remembered only to wonder that he should ever have mistaken it for real love. It was a very milk and water feeling contrasted with the madness that possessed him now.

Yet what to do? His orders were imperative and he must obey them to the last jot and tittle. Nothing must be allowed to prevent his reaching Berlin and delivering his packet to Rutile; nothing must be allowed to prevent him from reporting on board the Nevada at Brindisi four days later; and nothing must prevent him from reaching Japan and trying to get the information his government desired.

For the first time in his life the collar galled. Oh! to be free to take this woman in his arms and tell her that he loved her. He believed that he would not do so in vain. But he knew, none better, that he had no right to speak while bound for the antipodes. And if he could not speak he had no right to hint nor suggest nor attempt, however vaguely, to bind the girl's fancy.

For another reason he was not free. His mysterious illness had not recurred, but neither had it been explained. Several times he had seen and twice he had spoken with his Spanish-American acquaintance, (whose name turned out to be Sebastian Gomez), but he had been able to find out nothing suspicious about him. And even if he had been convinced of the man's guilt, he was still absolutely without reason to suspect Miss Ferreira of any complicity in it. Almost he had made up his mind that his illness had really been accidental. If his own interests alone had been concerned he would have dismissed the incident from his mind.

But not only his own interests were involved. His country had trusted him to carry a message safely to Berlin and he had no right to take any chance nor to neglect any precaution nor to disregard any threat, however slight, that might endanger his carrying out its behests. Until that packet was in Rutile's hands, he must not involve himself with anyone—least of all with anyone on whom even the suggestion of suspicion could fall.

So he kept silent, even on the last evening of the voyage—even when he saw the sun rise beyond the distant line that marked Germany and the port of Cuxhaven, at the mouth of the Elbe, where he must leave the ship and finish his journey to Berlin by rail, to the destruction of all chance for further familiar intercourse. He had resolved on his course and he would stick to it at whatever cost. He would part from the girl without a word of love and discharge his duty to the last iota. Then—then he would get leave or resign if need be and come back to seek her. It was cold comfort to hope that he might find her still free, but it was all he had.

Rapidly Cuxhaven swelled in the perspective, and soon the steamer drew alongside the dock. As Topham watched the welcoming crowd, Miss Ferreira, standing by his side, gave a cry and began to wave her handkerchief. "See, senor!" she exclaimed. "My brother! Yonder! Herrman! Herrman!" she called.

A patch of white fluttered in the hands of a man on the pier; and the owner pressed forward, eager to get on board. Soon Topham saw him coming up the plank.

The navy officer drew aside to let sister and brother meet without intrusion. Later, Miss Ferreira called him and he stepped forward to be introduced.

Ferreira was very like his sister, but was tall and strong, almost as tall and strong, Topham judged, as he himself. He clasped the American's hand warmly.

"I am delighted to meet you, senor," he cried. "My sister tells me how much you have done to make her crossing pleasant. Do you go directly to Berlin, senor?"

Topham nodded. "Directly!" he replied.

"Then we shall be fellow passengers."

"That will be pleasant. You came to take Miss Ferreira back, I suppose?"

But the Brazilian shook his head. "Not exactly," he replied. "I came to bring her word that she must stop over in Hamburg, only two hours away. Beyond Hamburg we will go on without her."

Without noticing that Topham had paled at his words the Brazilian glanced over the side.

"If you are ready, senor," he remarked, turning back. "Perhaps we had better descend to the custom house."

Topham hesitated. "If you'll wait for just an instant," he answered. "I'll be with you. I want to speak to the purser."

Ferreira nodded, and Topham disappeared. In a few minutes he was back. A slight bulge above his right breast showed the presence of a packet of some kind and an occasional slight lift of his coat in the fresh breeze, showed that it consisted of a big official-looking envelope.

But if either Ferreira or his sister noticed it they did not let the fact appear.

CHAPTER IV

The ride to Hamburg was short and pleasant. There the whole party disembarked; Elsa and the Baroness to remain, and Ferreira and Topham to take another train for Berlin.

In the waiting-room Topham made his farewells. Ferreira had gone to see after the baggage and the Baroness had fallen a little behind, so that the two were practically alone. Briefly, almost coldly, for fear his passion might break away in spite of himself, Topham pressed the girl's hand and bade her adieu.

"Good-by, Senorita," he said, slowly. "I have to thank you for a very delightful voyage. Is there no chance at all that I may see you in Berlin. I shall be there till day after tomorrow."

The girl shook her head. If she were piqued by Topham's self-restraint she did not show it. "I must stay in Hamburg for the present," she answered, deliberately. "I shall not go to Berlin till much later. So this is really good-by, senor."

"Good-by." Topham clasped her extended hand; then turned away, afraid to trust himself further.

But the girl called him back. "Senor!" she exclaimed softly. "Senor!"

"Yes!"

"Listen! Be careful. Be very careful. Things—happen—to strangers sometimes. Be very careful, senor, till you are safe in Berlin."

Topham stared. "I don't understand," he said.

"There is nothing to understand—except to be—careful. This country is not always altogether safe for strangers. Be careful—for my sake, senor."

The girl's voice broke and Topham started forward, flinging resolutions to the wind.

"Elsa," he cried. "I—"

But the voice of Ferreira broke in. "Cab's waiting, Elsa," he called. "Come along! Hurry! Or you'll make Senor Topham and me miss our train."

Recalled to himself by the interruption, Topham raised the girl's hand to his lips, then dropped it and saw her led away.

Soon Ferreira was back. "Quick, Senor Topham!" he called. "The train's waiting."

Many people apparently were going to Berlin, but few of them appeared to hold first-class tickets, and the two young men speedily found an empty carriage, in which they ensconced themselves.

Ferreira promptly leaned out of the window. "Here! guard," he said, holding out his hand. "I don't want to be bothered with other people! You understand!" A piece of silver changed hands and the Brazilian settled back.

Then he turned and nodded to Topham.

"We'll try to keep this compartment to ourselves, senor," he said. "I detest travelling shut in with three or four others. I suppose you agree with me."

Topham answered that he did.

An instant later the guards began to run along the platform slamming the doors. Just before they reached the carriage that sheltered Topham, two Germans came running up. One of them grabbed the handle of the door and jerked it open, and both precipitated themselves into the carriage, despite the Brazilian's strenuous protests.

"We have as good right here as you, nicht wahr?" asserted the foremost, seating himself without any ceremony. "This carriage is not reserved? What? It has no placard out? No!"

Ferreira fumed, pouring out so swift a torrent of guttural German that Topham, good German scholar as he was, could not understand one word in five. The intruders, however, clearly understood very well. Scornfully indifferent at first, they soon roused to the assault and apparently gave back as good as he sent.

In the middle of the dispute the train started, but neither Ferreira nor his adversary seemed to note that the case was closed. Hotter and hotter waxed the wordy war. Soon the two men were glaring at each other, shaking their fists and seeming on the point of flying at each other's throats.

Topham watched the contest with twinkling eyes. If he had been in Italy or France, where men are supposed to be more excitable, the scene would not have seemed very strange to him. But that notoriously phlegmatic Germans should work themselves into a passion over such a trifle seemed to him amazing. He scarcely believed, however, that the quarrel would end in actual violence; and so, though ready to aid Ferreira (Elsa's brother) if need arose, he sat still and looked on, letting a ghost of a smile flicker across his lips.

Instantly, with bewildering abruptness the other German leaned across the carriage, shaking his fist in the American's face, and shouting something which Topham did not catch, but which he instinctively knew was insulting.

The navy officer flushed angrily, and the next moment the other launched a blow at his face.

Topham parried and struck back shrewdly. He landed, but before he could follow up his advantage, the other German precipitated himself upon him, and in an instant the carriage became a pandemonium of struggling, kicking, fighting men.

Topham was big and strong, but he had been taken unawares, and found himself pinned down in the seat in the grasp of men stronger than he. Ferreira, though he struggled, did so ineffectively, and both intruders were practically free to concentrate on the American. The bout ended with Topham and Ferreira on the floor with the two Germans sitting on top of them, panting.

The struggle had lasted for some time, and in the momentary hush that followed its cessation the shriek of the locomotive was heard, whistling for a stop.

None of the four moved as the train slowed down. Then the Germans stood up, releasing the others. "We leave here, Herren," said the leader. "This is our address if you wish to carry matters further." They both bowed, flung down their cards, and stepped out through the door that the guard opened for them.

Left alone, Ferreira and Topham arose slowly. Topham was humiliated and intensely angry, but he saw the futility of engaging in a further contest at that moment. In fact, he scarcely knew what to do. The crisis had come with such bewildering suddenness, and had been so surprising both in its inception and its results, that it had taken away his breath, both actually and figuratively. That such a thing should happen in a German railway carriage, of all places in the world, was to him almost too amazing for belief.

Meanwhile Ferreira had snatched up the cards. "They shall die for this," he hissed. "Madre de Dios! But they shall die. I have friends here. They will act for you too, Senor Topham! Come! Let us seek them!" He made as if to leave the train.

But Topham shook his head. "Not for me," he declared. "I don't fight duels, not when I'm on duty, anyhow. Besides, I see little cause. They bested us fairly. Anyhow, it's too late now."

As a matter of fact, the train was moving again.

The Brazilian hesitated. Then suddenly he tore the cards to pieces and flung them out of the window. "So be it, Senor!" he acceded.

Topham glanced down at his clothes and found them whole, though badly rumpled. Suddenly he started, just as he had on the steamer the night he left New York, and thrust his hands into his inner pocket; then dropped it weakly to his side.

At his blank look Ferreira cried out: "You are hurt, senor!" he exclaimed.

Slowly the color came back to Topham's face. "No!" he said. "Not—not—hurt! You—you don't see an envelope—a big blue envelope—lying around anywhere, do you?" Dazedly he peered under the seats.

Ferreira aided him. "I hope it was not valuable, senor!" he ventured.

Slowly Topham shook his head. "Not intrinsically," he answered. "But—but it was—of great personal value to me. Those men must have taken it. I suppose it is too late to find them?"

The Brazilian looked blank. "Dolt that I am!" he cried. "I destroyed the cards!"

Topham nodded. "Probably they would be useless, anyhow," he muttered. "We will say no more about it, senor, if you will be so kind."

The rest of the trip passed uneventfully. Topham was moody and said little, and Ferreira did not disturb him.

When Berlin was reached Ferreira leaped lightly from the train. "You will come to my hotel, and refresh yourself, senor; it is not so?" he invited.

But Topham shook his head. "Thank you," he replied. "I must go first to the American Embassy. The secretary there is an old friend of mine. In fact I came by Berlin particularly to see him. So you will excuse me, senor."

Ferreira bowed. "Ah!" he exclaimed. "El Senor Rutile! He is a friend of yours? A fine fellow, Rutile! Boni! I shall do myself the honor to call on you later. Auf wiedersehen, senor."

With a nod and a bow he was gone.

Topham stared after him perplexedly. "I guess you were in it, my friend," he syllabled, slowly; "and I guess you think you've won. But the game isn't yours yet, not by a long shot." He paused; then "God bless her," he muttered. "She tried to save me! God bless her!"

CHAPTER V

"By Jove! Walter! I'm glad to see you." Rutile sprang to his feet and hurried forward as Topham entered the office of the embassy. "How are you, old man?" he rattled on. "I heard you were coming, but didn't expect you quite so soon. Must have had a quick trip!"

Topham shook hands, smilingly. No sign of distress on account of the missing papers clouded his eyes.

"Pretty quick," he answered. "Glad to get here; however."

Rutile turned. "Let me present you to the ambassador," he said. "Your Excellency! This is Mr. Topham of the navy, an old friend of mine, en route to Tokio via Brindisi and Suez."

Topham started and shot a glance of surprise at Rutile. Then he turned back to the ambassador, who smiled and put out his hand.

"I'm glad to see you, Mr. Topham," he said, a little ponderously. "Isn't it er—rather unusual to go from Washington to Tokio by way of Berlin?"

The ambassador's tones were entirely casual, but Topham thought he detected some veiled meaning in them, perhaps because he was thinking of the secretary's caution to say nothing to the ambassador about the papers placed in his charge. "Well! yes! it is unusual," he answered. "You see the navy's short of officers and has to make out as best it can. They are going to make me earn my passage to Tokio by serving as watch officer on the Nevada. She leaves Brindisi for Manila on Friday, and I'm to join her, so as to let one of her present officers be invalided home."

"But even so, Berlin seems off your route."

Topham laughed. "It is a little," he assented. "But I had never been here and I wanted to see old Rutile, and so I persuaded the personnel bureau to make my orders read via Berlin. It isn't much out of the way."

"I see!" The ambassador rose. "I—er—thought at first that you might have brought me some special instructions?" His voice had a slight rising inflection at the end.

But Topham shook his head. "Nothing of the sort, I'm sorry to say, Your Excellency," he replied.

"No? It's just as well. Special instructions are usually unpleasant. I'll be glad to see you at my house if your engagements will allow, Mr. Topham." He turned to the secretary. "Just send my mail in to me, will you, Mr. Rutile?" he finished.

Rutile turned to a pile of mail that had evidently just been dumped on the table. "Here are two letters for you right on top," he remarked, passing them over. "If I find any more, I'll send them in."

"Do!Mr. Topham, since you have come so far to see Mr. Rutile, I won't interfere with your chat with him any longer."

The ambassador looked from one young man to the other and his eyes twinkled; but he left the room with nothing more except a nod.

As soon as he was gone, Rutile turned to Topham. "Well! Let's have it, old man!" he exclaimed.

Topham did not answer at once. He had drawn near the table and was staring at the pile of mail matter. "So this is how you get your mail," he remarked, with apparent irrelevance.

"That! Oh! that isn't official mail! That's mostly letters and papers for tourists sent in care of the embassy. The official mail comes in a private bag. But let's have those instructions."

Topham's eyebrows went up! "What instructions?" he demanded.

"The instructions you brought me from the Secretary of State, of course."

"Oh! * * * How do you know I have any special instructions for you?"

"The department tipped it off by cable! Let's have 'em."

But Topham shook his head. "Hold on a minute!" he exclaimed. "I should like to understand this game, if you are at liberty to explain. Why in thunder is the Secretary of State sending you instructions by a navy officer instead of by the regular channels, and why is he sending you any instructions at all that he conceals from the ambassador?"

Rutile threw himself back in the chair. "Search me!" he replied cheerfully. "'These are the Lord's doings; they are wonderful in our sight!' If I had to guess, though, I should say that the instructions you bring treat of a secret service matter which has nothing to do with ambassadorial duties—yet."

"I don't understand."

"Of course not. But it's like this! Ambassadors are usually highly polished, highly educated, highly ornate somebodies who have the money and the wish to put up a fine front. Their principal duties are to cultivate people, give dinners, and generally jolly things along. Besides, they come and go, and can't be expected to know all the ins and outs of the game. We secretaries are more permanent, and we are expected to know it all—and to plan it. If we make a slip, the ambassador disavows us, and we are recalled. We are denounced as presumptuous underlings who have acted without authority—not worth quarreling over. Do you understand now?"

Topham nodded. "Yes! I begin to understand," he said.

"All right! Now let's have the papers."

But Topham shook his head. "I haven't any papers for you, Rutile!" he said soberly. "I did have, but—I haven't now!"

Rutile stared at him. "Good Lord! Man! You haven't lost them, have you?" he cried.

Topham hesitated. "No!" he answered, at last. "I haven't lost them. But I became a little alarmed about their safety and so I put them into an envelope and addressed them to John Smith in care of the embassy here. I carried a dummy in my pocket. The purser said they would reach here about as soon as I did, and unless I am mistaken they are in that envelope close to your hand on the table there. Allow me!"

The navy officer reached over and picked up an envelope. He opened it and took out a packet which he handed to Rutile.

"Take your instructions," he said.

Rutile threw himself back in his chair. "Well! I'm d—d!" he observed.

"Very likely!"

"But—but why did you— What happened to—"

"Nothing! Nothing at all! There were some slight incidents—nothing of any importance."

"Oh! Nothing of any importance. Humph!" Rutile's tones were sarcastic; but he understood that for some reason Topham did not wish to speak frankly, and so he proceeded cautiously.

"Er—voyage quite pleasant, I suppose?" he questioned.

Topham laughed ruefully. "Oh! Yes," he answered, slowly. "Yes! Very pleasant. Delightful, in fact! But, confound it, old man! Do you know, I was seasick? Think of it! Seasick! Why, I haven't been seasick for ten years—not since my maiden cruise in Academy days. But I got it this time good and proper!"

"Ah!" Rutile dropped his eyes, and began playing with a paper weight. "How long did it last?" he questioned, carefully.

"Couple of days! It caught me right after dinner the first night out. I went really dizzy. Fortunately it was cloudy and there weren't any people on deck, and my shameful secret became known to few. A girl who happened to be there offered me a chair and I lay in it till I could get to my cabin."

"Humph! It's lucky you didn't go to sleep in that chair—with these papers in your pocket!"

"I did go to sleep. Had quite a—er—nap, I suspect. But the papers weren't in my pocket. The purser had them in his safe."

"Oh! I see!" Rutile laughed shortly. "Of course your humiliating experience spoiled any chance for a flirtation with the charming girl who—she was charming, of course."

"She was, emphatically!"

"What was her name?"

"Miss Elsa Ferreira!"

"What!"

"Miss Elsa Ferreira. Do you know her?"

"Do I? Well—But that can't be all. Were there any more—er—incidents?"

"Well, yes!" Topham spoke carefully. "Yes. There was one other small occurrence. I came up from Cuxhaven with her brother."

"Ah! You were—alone—with him?"

"Only for a few minutes. Two other men insisted on butting into our compartment. Ferreira got quite excited in his efforts to keep them out, but they would come in. Of course, they had as much right as we did. But Ferreira wouldn't stand for it and actually came to blows with them. In fact I was involved and—I got the worst of it, too!"

With a chuckle Rutile threw himself back in his chair. "Well! I will be d—d!" he observed. "You don't mean you had a regular fight, do you?"

Topham grinned. "Well! Not exactly. The intruders simply sat down on Ferreira and me. We weren't in it, really. Then at the next stop they threw down their cards and left the train."

"Their cards? What were their names?"

"I don't know! Ferreira—by the way, he said he knew you—Ferreira—er—lost them out of the window!" replied Topham, guilelessly. "Later I discovered that somehow I had lost my dummy package in the scuffle."

"Oh! Oh!—And the lady? What became of her?"

"She stayed in Hamburg. You understand, old man, these things that I've been telling you are mere incidents of travel, of no real consequence. You do understand that, don't you?"

Rutile choked. "Oh! yes! certainly," he acceded. "Now, if you'll excuse me for a moment I'll see just what these instructions are about."

"All right!"

Rutile examined the carefully placed seals, made sure that they were intact, and then broke them and drew out the papers inside. A moment later he gave a low whistle.

"Say, old man?" he exclaimed. "It's just as I thought. You came over with—with—"

The sentence was never finished. While the secretary hesitated for a word, the door of the room was flung open and a young man rushed in and dropped into a chair.

CHAPTER VI

The young man who flung into the embassy as if he owned it was small, round and jolly, with a twinkle in his eye that persisted even when, as at the moment in question, he was fuming with anger and disgust.

"Give me a drink, for God's sake, Rutile," he cried. "I've been talking to Ouro Preto and I need a bracer. Of all the—"

"Hello, Risdon!" Topham stepped forward and held out his hand. "Hello! old man!" he repeated, smilingly.

"By all the gods! Walter Topham! Where in thunder did you come from?" He grabbed the other's hand and wrung it warmly. "Say!" he went on, "We've simply got to celebrate this! Rutile. Are you going to order those drinks, or shall I?"

Rutile was again looking through the papers brought by Topham. Without raising his eyes he reached over and pounded a bell. "Shut up or talk to Topham till I finish this," he ordered.

"What you reading? A love letter?"

"Lord! no! Nothing half so important. Only some stuff from the State Department."

"Oh! That! Let it go!" He turned back to Topham. "By George old man! I haven't seen you since I bilged from the U. S. N. A. Who'd a-thought we three would ever meet here? You, the savey man of the class; Rutile, the—the—I'll be darned if I know what; and me the only one of the three who's done a lick of work since we got out of the Academy—and then only because Uncle Sam gently but firmly refused to support me. But, say, Topham! How'd you get here? In command of a canal boat? Why don't you speak up instead of making a quiet man break his rule against talking?"

Topham smiled. In fact, he had been smiling ever since he clasped Risdon's hand, quite content to let the other rattle on unchecked. But at Risdon's direct appeal, he began to speak, only to pause as a darkey servant thrust his head in the door.

Rutile glanced up. "Three beers, Caesar," he ordered, and resumed his writing.

"Three beers!" protested Risdon, disgustedly. "Good Heavens! Rutile! Three beers! And you claim to be from Kentucky." Then, seeing that the secretary was not listening, he turned again to Topham.

"Where'd you say you were going to?" he demanded.

"I didn't say. But I'm on my way to Tokio as naval attaché. Leave here tomorrow night; join the Nevada at Brindisi Friday; go with her to Manila as watch officer and then by passenger steamer to Japan. Stopped over here a day to see Rutile."

Caesar re-entered with the beer, but with him he brought a tall dark bottle and three small glasses. "Ain't goin' to offer beer to no navy officer or newspaper gen'mens", he muttered. "Ain't a-going to do it, nohow, massa Rutile."

Rutile grinned and laid down his papers. "Help yourselves, fellows!" he said. "Maybe Caesar knows your tastes better than I do. Prosit!" He lifted his stein and gulped the liquid. "Now, Risdon," he went on, "You may confide your troubles to Uncle Sam. What's troubling the special commissioner of the New York Gazette to his Imperial Majesty Wilhelm and the other crowned heads of Europe, Asia, and Africa?"

An expression of disgust came over the correspondent's face. "Don't be funny," he said, severely. "If you think staggering under that tom-fool appellation is any joke you're mistaken. Say! Rutile! What do you think of that fellow Ouro Preto, anyhow? Reveal your inmost soul—not necessarily for publication, but as an evidence of good sense. Speak the truth. There are no ladies present, so you needn't restrain yourself."

Rutile stretched out his legs and grinned. "I don't like Ouro Preto much myself," he answered; "but plenty of others do. What's he done to you?"

"It isn't what he's done; its what he is! He's always making up to me—God knows what for. I don't like him."

"Natural antipathy, eh! Ouro Preto is a half German, half Brazilian count, Topham, who's spending the winter in Berlin and who's trod on Risdon's toes somehow. Probably refused to admit the right of the American press to pry into his inmost concerns."

"Refused, nothing!" shouted the reporter. "It's my business to read men, and it ought to be yours, Rutile, if you were with your salt. We're all as God made us, if not worse. But I give you fair warning to watch out for Ouro Preto. He'll do you dirt if he gets the chance."

Rutile did not laugh, though he looked as though he would much have liked doing so. The correspondent's rhodomontade did not seem to impress him greatly. "And the villain still pursued her," he remarked, casually.

"Oh! all right. Go your own way. Only don't say I didn't warn you. I'm not the only one who thinks so. If it wasn't for his sister he'd be kicked out mucho pronto! Say! Topham! You never met his sister, did you?"

Topham shook his head but did not speak.

"Well! You don't want to! Not if you've got a girl back home and want to remember her. The countess catches all sorts and every sort. She's the prettiest, wittiest, beautifulest—"

Before Topham could shape an answer, a passing band struck up one of the waltzes of the day, and with its strains there rose before the navy officer's mind a face—the face of the girl with whom he had sat upon the steamer two nights before and listened to the band play that same waltz.

The music died away in the distance, and he looked up at Risdon. "When's the wedding to be?" he laughed.

"The wedding? God forbid! I'd as soon marry a catamount. Not that this particular catamount would marry me or any one else less than a duke—if she and that brother of hers get what they're after. But that doesn't make her any the less entertaining—when she has something to gain by it. She worked me all right—once." The correspondent winced at the recollection. "Wait till you see her!"

"Probably I won't. I must be off tomorrow, you know. Who are they—she and her brother—anyway? And what are they after?"

"After? Trouble! Big trouble sure! Rutile won't admit it—for publication. Says I'm a yellow reporter, you know. But it's so, all the same. But, say, I've got to go up to the war office. Come along with me and I'll tell you the yarn!"

"Yes! Do! Go along, Topham. I've got an hour's work that must be done, and then I'm at your service. And—by the way, when you cross the bridge, pick Risdon up by the nape of the neck and drop him gently into the River Spree. Then come back to lunch."

Risdon jumped up. "That's American bluntness, I suppose," he exclaimed. "Ouro Preto said the other day that Americans had no more manners than a wet dog. I came near knocking him down for it, but I'll be darned if I don't believe he was right. Come along, Topham."

The two young men clattered down the stairs into the broad Unter den Linden. Crowds thronged the sidewalk and a double current of miscellaneous vehicles moved unceasing between the curbs. Everything on wheels was represented, from a 60-horsepower automobile to an oxcart. Laughing and chatting Risdon led Topham through the maze, pointing out famous men and famous places with comments, the least of which, if overheard by any one of the stiff-necked German officers they passed, would have brought forth an immediate challenge.

After a while he pointed to an ornate stone pile. "That's where our pretty countess lives," he remarked, airily. "I haven't seen her for two or three weeks. Wonder where she's keeping herself?"

"The countess Ouro Preto? Oh! yes! You were going to tell me something about her, weren't you?" questioned Topham, carelessly.

"Sure! * * * it's this way. She and her brother are the children of the Count Ouro Preto, Governor of the state of Rio Grande do Sul, Brazil. They are also the grandchildren of a former Duke of Hochstein, by a second, morganatic, marriage with a ballet dancer, by whom he had one daughter. All the duke's children by his first and royal consort died. All his nephews died. Everybody died, except the morganatic daughter, who married a Brazilian, the Count of Ouro Preto, and went to South America with him. The ducal line became extinct, for of course this daughter's descendants had no standing. Now comes Ouro Preto and his sister, children of this daughter, backed by enormous wealth, and petition the Emperor to revive the duchy in their behalf. You see, her marriage to the duke was proper and religious and all that, and was only morganatic because the duke was chief of a mediatized German house, and couldn't marry except among his princely beery peers. Now the Ouro Pretos have faked up a royal pedigree for the ballet dancer. If they can make it stick, they establish her moral claim to the duchy, and gain a sort of backstairs standing for themselves. Of course the ballet dancer pedigree is faked; everybody says it's faked; the Kaiser probably knows it's faked; but that won't cut any ice if Wilhelm decides to declare it established. And everybody is on pins and needles to know whether he is going to do it or not. Ouro Preto has offered to buy back the ducal estates, which were escheated to the Emperor half a century ago, at two million dollars, which is about three times their value, and to spend two million more on beautifying the tiny capital of Hochstein. It's all a matter of price. Lord, Topham! I used to think we had a monopoly of graft on the other side of the water. But we haven't. Not a bit of it. We buy senatorships and these people buy titles. The same longing for power, the same craving for notoriety, the same love of display exists in the U. S. A. as here. Ouro Preto wants to be a sovereign duke and he's got the scads to pay for it. It's up to the kaiser to say whether he bids high enough. And I shouldn't wonder if the Countess Elsa would turn the scale."

Suddenly the reporter broke off. He clutched Topham by the arm and dragged him to the edge of the pavement. "Stand still a minute," he ordered, as he rested his hand on the navy officer's shoulder and raised himself on tiptoe. "Yes! it's she," he exclaimed, an instant later. "You big men will never realize how useful your inches are till you try being a little man in a crowd. You say you have never seen the fair Elsa, Countess del Ouro Preto? Well! You are about to have that pleasure. Yonder she comes, in that red motor."

Walter looked where the other pointed. Then something seemed to grip him by the throat, and he caught at the journalist's shoulder to steady himself.

The motor was very near, and he could see its occupants distinctly. They were two in number. One was stout and middleaged; Topham's eyes passed over her unheeding. The other was Elsa Ferreira.

Her eyes met Topham's and a great wave of crimson flooded over her cheeks. Her hand slipped, and the motor swerved sharply. The other woman started and screamed out, and the fair driver, suddenly recalled to herself, barely avoided a collision. Then the car swept on.

Topham followed it with his eyes, forgetful of his whereabouts till it was swallowed up in the press. Then suddenly he became aware that the correspondent was shaking him violently by the arm.

"What is it?" he questioned vaguely.

"What is it!" Risdon's voice was trembling with excitement. "What is it? Brace up, for God's sake, Walter," he begged. "People are staring. If you could see yourself! But good Lord, I don't wonder! Nobody ever looked at me as that woman looked at you."

With a great effort Topham regained his composure. "Nonsense!" he said. "Forget for a moment that you're a yellow journalist, Risdon, and don't try to make a sensation out of nothing. I know the lady slightly. She crossed with me from New York."

CHAPTER VII

Topham never remembered how he got through the next hour. He went from place to place with Risdon, talked and laughed, met men—some of them famous men, too—but he did it all mechanically. His thoughts were with the girl whom he had seen in the automobile—the girl with whom he had crossed from New York—the girl who had told him her name was Elsa Ferreira—the girl who had warned him to be careful. Clearly she was one of the conspirators against himself, but he did not care. He had given the letter safely to Risdon and was free to act for himself for twenty-four hours—till it was time to leave Berlin.

When at last the hour for luncheon was at hand and he could leave Risdon on a plea that he must hurry back to the embassy, he did so with an alacrity which he feared the reporter would detect.

Once alone he lost no time in making his way to the ornate stone pile that Risdon had pointed out to him as the home of the Count and Countess of Ouro Preto.

Scarcely could he control himself while he waited for a reply to the card he sent up. It seemed to him incredible that it had been only that morning that he had parted from Elsa—he thought of her as Elsa—at the steamer. It seemed weeks even since he had gazed into her eyes across the traffic that thronged the street.

By and by a man came down the stairs. Topham recognized him as his Spanish-American acquaintance of the cigarette episode and grinned. "They're all in it," he observed. "But I don't care. I don't care a continental damn."

He turned as a trim maid servant came running down the stairs, and bowed before him.

"The wohlgebornen Grafin will receive the Herr Lieutenant Topham," she said. "Be pleased to walk up!"

Topham did so without delay.

As he entered her apartment the countess rose, and for an instant the two stared at each other. Curiosity was in that gaze, for those two had learned much about each other since they had parted. Defiance was in it, for both felt instinctively that their wills were to clash and both were ready for the encounter; fascination—or something strangely akin to fascination—was in it. The pause was that of two fencers who hesitate before they cross swords.

It was for a second only, then the countess swept forward and held out her hand. "Mr. Topham?" she murmured. "I am glad to see you."

Topham bowed as he took the hand in his. She wore a wonderful gown of clinging silk against which her dark beauty scintilated star-like. He could not speak. Her loveliness and what it meant—must mean—to him in the future took his breath away and held him for the moment dumb.

"But you ought not to have come!" she went on, slowly, when he did not speak.

Topham shook his head. "You knew I would come," he declared, meaningly.

The countess flushed, and Topham pushed the fight. "Did you not know it?" he demanded.

Changing emotion swept across the countess's mobile face. Surprise, indignation, panic succeeded each other and at last gave place to an expression hard to define. She flushed, trembled slightly; and her eyes dropped before those of the man who still held her hand.

"Yes!" she breathed. "Yes! I knew."

"Ahem!" An elderly lady had risen and came forward and seemed somewhat amazed by the scene. "Ahem! Ahem!" she coughed, and then more violently, "Ahem!"

The countess started. One would have said that she had forgotten her companion, which was singular for a girl brought up under the duenna system, however much she might have emancipated herself. Then she turned. "You know the Baroness Ostersacken, Mr. Topham," she said.

Topham bowed. "Yes!" he said. "I know."

"Ach! Gott!" The baroness seemed confused. "You are welcome, Herr Topham," she declared. "Will you not be seated?"

The countess led the way to a window beside which two chairs were placed, while the baroness, waddling back to the seat some distance away, from which she had risen, picked up some fancy work.

The countess sat down and indicated the chair by her side. "Sit down, Mr. Topham," she invited.

But Topham stood motionless, hand on the back of the chair, looking at her.

The sun streamed golden through the great window, a stray beam lighting on her hair, transformed its dark mass into iridescent fire. A potted palm swept her shoulders with its delicate fronds. From the street below came up the tramp of men, the rattle of wagons, the jingle of a tram car.

Abruptly Topham spoke. "Please send the baroness away!" he directed, serenely.

Again the countess' face flamed. She rose half way from her chair; then sat down again, trembling.

"Senor!" she faltered, returning instinctively to her mother tongue. "What mean you? I—I can not receive you without a duenna. It—it is impossible."

"Not to you! To others, perhaps! Send her away—please."

"But it is impos—" She rose. "Baroness," she said, "would you mind looking for a letter from Herrman that I left in the bottom of my escritoire?"

The baroness rose. Her expression was inscrutable. Perhaps she was already so much surprised that her features, incapable of expressing her amazement, had reverted to their former placidity—a placidity from which nothing was likely soon to stir them. "Yes! Yes!" she murmured. "Yes! Yes! Mein Gott!"

When she had disappeared through the door at the end of the room the countess turned to Topham. "Now, senor," she said, with more spirit than she had shown since the American's arrival. "I have obeyed your orders and sent away my duenna. True, she is only in the next room, but still we are alone. What have you to say to me to warrant such a demand?"

"You know." Topham's voice was not quite so steady. "Senorita," he went on. "Let me tell you something of myself. I belong to an old Virginia family— one of the F. F. Vs., as they call us derisively. My people have lived in Virginia for nearly three hundred years, and nearly every one of them had a romance. My great grandparents eloped; my grandfather married my grandmother the day after he met her; my father wanted to marry my mother at first sight of her, but was compelled to wait a year—till he was nineteen. I understand that your heritage is similar; that your father stole your mother from the duke's palace. Finally"—He paused and leaned forward.

"When I parted from you this morning I thought I could wait. I meant to see you again, but I thought—. But I was wrong. I can not leave you without speaking! When I saw you on the street I knew that I could not. Love has come to me suddenly, as it comes to all the men of my race—suddenly but for all time. I have played at love-making before. I did not know what love was. I thought—Good God! How could I have thought as I did? How could any man mistake water for wine, moonshine for sunshine?"

Very slowly and deliberately, he took the countess' face between his palms and looked down at her. "Look at me, Elsa," he said.

Slowly she lifted her starry eyes to his. He bent forward and their lips met. "That makes you mine," he said slowly.

The countess said not a word, but she slipped slowly into his arms and nestled against his broad bosom. It was preposterous, ridiculous, incredible—this love-making; it was "so very American", but—but—what the countess really thought about it would be hard to tell. Whether she was as mad as Topham or whether there was a purpose in her madness did not appear.

Topham tilted her perfect chin upward. "Doesn't it?" he asked, with a shade of anxiety in his voice. "You love me? You will marry me—soon?"

Gently the countess freed herself; then she stood up and faced him. "Yes!" she said. "I love you, and I will marry you or no other man," She stepped closer to him, and reaching up, placed both hands upon his shoulders and kissed him on the mouth. "Yes!" she repeated. "I will marry you—but not soon."

"Why not? I am under orders. I must leave Berlin tonight. Will you come with me—or shall I resign from the Navy and stay with you?"

"Neither! I can not marry you—now. No! That is not true! I can, but I will not. I dare not."

"Dare not! Who prevents—

"Honor!"

"Honor? Whose honor? yours?"

"No. Your own. What is mine? What is any woman's when she loves? And I do love. Do you understand? From the moment I saw you I loved you? I fought against it. I may not love any man—now; least of all, you. I am dangerous to you—dangerous! That is why I lied to you. That is why I told you that I was going to stop in Hamburg instead of coming to Berlin. It was by a mere chance that you saw me on the street. But I love you. I have never loved any man before nor will again. No other man has ever touched my lips. Do you believe me? No—don't answer. I know that you do. I love you, and I am careful of your honor—more careful that I would be of my own. Therefore, I will not marry you—soon."

Very straight she stood against the background of palms. Topham, slow of thought as he was, felt vaguely that she had stood thus rigid through life that bent around her. But he was determined, too. Stubbornness rose within him.

But before he could speak, she flung up her hand. "No! Don't say it!" she begged. "Don't compel me to yield. You could do it. No other man ever bent me; but you—you could break me. But it is best not to do it. Believe me, you will be sorry if—

"Look you, senor! For years I have lived for but one thing, and that thing is close to my hand. Yet I would give it up for you and count it gain to do so if others were not involved—others who rely on me—others to whom I have passed my word. And yet, I will give it up—if you ask me. What is a woman's word, after all? Shall I give it up?"

Topham shook his head. "Not if you have passed your word. My wife's word is mine!" he answered, with splendid egotism.

The countess smiled—but tenderly. Perhaps she noticed the egotism and was proud of it.

"Then," she said. "I can not marry you soon. It will take a full year to redeem my word; and until that is done I can not marry you. Perhaps"—her voice broke—"perhaps you will not want to marry me then. But God rules and I can not think he has brought you to me merely to take you away again."

She paused and clasped her hands above her heart. "You must not even see me during that year," she went on, painfully. "No! Believe me! I know best. It must be! Go to your ship and come back in a year—if you will. I, too, am going away soon. When the year is up, or sooner, if it be possible, I will let you know where I am. Then, if you care to come to me—"

"Come? I would—"

"Be not too sure. A year is a long time. No! I do not doubt you. But—but— Kiss me once more, Walter! On the lips! Kiss me! And then leave me, for this is good-by."

CHAPTER VIII

Topham and Rutile met at dinner that night, but neither touched on the subject that lay nearest the navy officer's heart. Topham was slow to tell his feelings at any time, and in this particular instance he wanted to think a little more before he made a confidant of any one. Rutile, on the other hand, did not care to attempt to force the other's confidence. So they talked the meal through on indifferent topics.

Dinner over, Rutile excused himself. "I'm awfully sorry, old man," he said. "But I find I can't be with you until late tonight. I've got about three hours of work that must be done, even if the heavens fall. I hate to leave you on your only night here, but—"

"Nonsense. That's all right! I know what orders are. I'll make out. I—well, I've got to think something out, myself, and I'll be glad of the chance. Just tell me where I can go and moon about—"

"Why not go out to the Thiergarten? The band will be playing and everybody will be there, but you can be as lonely as you please, if you please. Stay there a few hours and then show up at the embassy about eleven or twelve o'clock and we'll have a talk or go out and paint the town, whichever you like. Berlin isn't Paris, but it doesn't go to bed by curfew law, either."

"Thank you! I'll do as you say. But I don't care to incarnadine anything. How do I get to this Thiergarten place?"

Rutile told him and an hour later Topham was walking along the spacious roadways of the park, thinking of nearly everything but his surroundings.

He was twenty-five, clean-shaven, Gibsonesque, with the erect carriage that bespeaks military training. As he moved slowly through the crowd, many halted for a second and glanced at him before turning to the next corner in the kaleidoscopic throng. Two looks are the best compliment a stranger can pay; a single glance asserts insignificance, and three glances argue peculiarity. Walter Topham was neither insignificant nor peculiar.

But though many looked at Topham, he looked at nobody. The fair face of the Countess Elsa was ever before his mind's eye, filling it to the exclusion of all else. How could he live for a whole year without seeing her? How could he accept her orders as final? Yet what could he do? What could he do? He had been glad to get away from Rutile and that he might once more ask himself the question.

At the edge of the garden he paused and stared unseeingly down the long avenue stretched before him, hesitating whether or not to turn back. He cared little for his surroundings. Wherever he was, he saw only the brilliant tints of this Brazilian countess who wanted to become a German duchess.

Abruptly his mood changed; he wanted human companionship; and he faced back into the garden, vaguely wondering whether in its merry-making throngs he could find the escape from his own thoughts he craved.

The scene was a charming one. Beneath the radiant gaslights moved a vivid kaleidoscope of uniforms and gowns. Faces, now sternly handsome, now softly beautiful, flashed out and then disappeared. The animal houses, built after the fashion of the countries whence their occupants came, showed here and there through the trees—now an elephant house from India and next a pagoda filled with bright-colored Japanese birds. To Topham's ears as the music hushed, came the sound of gay laughter and happy song, mingled with the tinkling of glasses from the little tables beneath the trees. The air was heavy with the scent of flowers or perhaps with perfume shaken from the gowns of the women. The Berliners were making merry in the hearty whole-souled German way that forgets the toils of the day the moment they are over and recalls them only when the time comes to resume them.

Insensibly the spirit of the place calmed the American. "We've nothing like this at home," he mused, "More's the pity. We're too feverish, too anxious to finish, so as to be able to start again. Will we ever really finish, I wonder? Is it our climate or is it merely a passing phase of our character? We seem to drop out of it readily enough when we come over here. I don't suppose there is a soul in all this crowd that is thinking of anything except the pleasure of the moment."

He rested his hand on the back of a vacant chair and stared at the crowd. Hundreds of people were passing him every minute, but he knew none of them. He could not hope to see the countess, of course, and he cared little for any one else.

The fates, however, were propitious. Scarcely had he begun to watch, when he heard his name called. He looked up and smiled. It was Herrman Ferreira—he who had shared his compartment on the train, he whom he had come to identify with the Count del Ouro Preto. That is to say, it was the brother of his charmer—if not the rose it was the nearest thorn.

"Ah Herr Topham! Well found, my friend. You have quite recovered from the affair on the train?"

"Oh! Quite! And you?"

"But yes! I hope you have suffered no inconvenience from the loss of your papers?" The Brazilian's tones were light, but Topham thought he read a note of anxiety in them.

"Very little," he replied. "They were only of sentimental value, Count!"

"Count!" The other smiled. "Ah! Ha! You know. My good friend Rutile has told you? Yes! I am count. But I seldom use the title. I fly higher. Perhaps you have heard."

Topham nodded, and the Brazilian rattled on. "Boni!" he exclaimed. "I have good news. Come and rejoice with me. As you Americans say, come and smile with me." He caught Walter by the arm and drew him down the walk to the tables beneath the trees.

Topham went willingly enough. Despite the warning of the Gazette correspondent, he rather liked Ouro Preto. Besides, he was the brother of the Countess Elsa.

Ouro Preto picked out a table and beckoned to a waiter. "What will you have, my friend," he demanded, as he dropped into his chair. "The gin-rickey or the horse's-neck or the mint-julep of America; the wine of France; or the beer of Germany?"

"Anything, so long as it's beer," returned Topham, lightly. "But, Count, what's your good news?"

"The best ever. You know what it is I want in Berlin? Yes? Well, the Emperor will see me tomorrow at ten."

Walter caught up the stein which the swift-footed waiter had placed before him. "Congratulations!" he cried, and gulped the beer.

Ouro Preto nodded. His eyes were bright with excitement, and his dark cheeks burned with color. "That argues much, eh? friend Topham?" he questioned. "Wilhelm does not see a man in private audience unless he has something to say to him. If he meant to refuse, he could do so by proxy. That he consents to see me means—means—well, I scarcely dare guess what it may mean."

Walter played with his stein. "I'm not familiar with the Emperor's ways," he observed, "But to be received in private audience seems a mighty good augury."

Ouro Preto sipped his beer slowly. "It's great," he cried. "It must mean something. And yet you can never tell. Obstacles arise out of nothing. There are so many interlocking interests over here. One touches a Frenchman and a Russian suddenly springs up in his way. One whispers a secret to an Italian, and the next day an Englishman greets him with it. You Americans are happy to stand aside from all this. As the great Washington said, you have no entangling alliances. You need no diplomacy. But here—here every man must be a diplomat and must intrigue. It is of a necessity."

The Brazilian raised his stick and beckoned again to the waiter. "Zwei bier," he ordered. While he waited, he gazed round at the near-by tables, scanning their occupants one by one, as if to single out any who might be watching.

Those at the tables were sufficiently diverse. At one table a couple of Englishmen were drinking gin; at another the members of a party, conspicuously American, were laughing guiltily as they tasted unaccustomed wine; beyond two or three Italians were making a tremendous noise over a bottle of vin ordinaire; close at hand an unescorted lady, apparently French, was sipping a glass of champagne.

The count seemed satisfied with the results of his scrutiny, for he turned to Topham with a smile. "Only the usual set," he observed, "At least, so far as I can see. Probably I alarm myself needlessly. So far as I know, it is to no one's interest to oppose me. You can think of no one, eh! my friend?"

"I?" Topham stared at the man in surprise. "Of course not. I didn't know till today what you were after; and certainly I have never heard anyone suggest any opposition. Why should they?"

The Brazilian laughed. "Why should they, indeed?" he answered, lightly. He broke off, and Topham saw that he was watching some one.

The swish of a skirt just behind his chair and a faint perfume that stole upon his senses warned the American not to look around too suddenly. When he did manage to turn with sufficient casualness, he saw two ladies and a gentleman taking their seats at a vacant table a few feet away. The man's face was toward him and he recognized him at once. The girls' backs were turned, but something familiar in the pose of one of them set his heart to thumping.

Ouro Preto leaned forward, excitedly. "Do you know who they are?" he demanded. "The ladies, I mean. I know the ambassador, of course, though only by sight."

Topham nodded. "I know one of them," he declared. "One is Lord Maxwell's daughter. The other—"

But the Brazilian was not listening. "Did you see her face?" he questioned. "Hers! The one to the right. She's a wonderful creature! Dios! Topham! I must meet her!"

Topham was still staring at the back of the girl who seemed familiar. Surely it could not be—and yet—

She wore a wide basket hat, from beneath which little yellow tendrils tumbled, shining red gold against her slender white neck. Topham was sure he had seen those curls against that neck before. The delicate poise of her head, too, was familiar. If she would only turn her head a trifle—She did it, and Topham rose quickly to his feet. "Lillian!" he gasped.

Ouro Preto's voice reached his ear. "Do you know her?" he asked. "Can you present me?"

Topham nodded. "Certainly! If she will give me permission," he answered. "Please excuse me while I recall myself to her."

CHAPTER IX

Topham's heart was light as he approached the table of the new arrivals. Lillian Byrd was the last person he had expected to see in Berlin. He had supposed her 3000 miles away at her home in Washington. He had not seen her for two years—not since the day that she had refused to marry him. He had known her pretty nearly all his life, but he had not thought of her as a possible sweetheart until the day when she had come back to her Washington home from college and met him there on his first assignment to Washington duty after leaving Annapolis.

Deliberate in all things else, he, like all the men of his family, was impetuous in love; and he had spoken to her almost at once. She had laughed at him, but in a way that invited further pursuit. In fact, he told himself she had deliberately kept him in tow until she could find someone better. Unattached young men were scarce in Washington, and few girls had a good-looking young naval officer utterly to themselves; and Miss Byrd did not care to lose her cavalier. For the whole of one Washington season she kept him; but when she came back the next fall after a summer at Newport, she had changed. Perhaps it was because she had made many more friends; perhaps it was because she had made some one particular friend; at any rate, she did not care so much for his attention—and she showed it. He reproached her, and demanded immediate acceptance or final rejection. He got rejection, and instantly applied for sea duty, hoping that absence would ease the pain.

Two years at sea had not made him forget. Either the lack of congenial friends or something that struck deeper had kept her face always before him. And then, in a day, in a moment, it had dimmed.

It seemed to Topham a very wonderful thing that he should meet her again, at almost the moment when he had first seen another woman whose image had effaced hers. For he no longer doubted what had happened to him that afternoon.

He passed by her chair, then faced her and raised his hat.

"Good-evening, Miss Byrd," he said, smilingly. With perfect self-possession, the girl stared at him; then she held out her hand with a glad smile.

"Lieutenant Topham!" she exclaimed, with sparkling eyes. "Oh! I *am* glad." That was ever the way with Lillian Byrd; the little emphasis in her tones always singled out the one addressed and made him feel himself the most important person in her world.

"Let me present you to Lord Maxwell," she went on, warmly. "This is Lieutenant Topham of the United States Navy, Lord Maxwell," she finished, with a flash of her marvellous eyes.

Lord Maxwell rose and held out his hand. "I already have the pleasure of Mr. Topham's acquaintance," he declared. "My daughter, Ellen, Mr. Topham."

Topham bowed, and his lordship went on. "We are about to sample an American drink, Mr. Topham," he said, "One highly recommended by Miss Byrd. It is, I believe, known as ice cream soda. Of course, it is prepared here à la German, and I can not speak as to its merits. Will you sit down and tempt fate with us?"

Walter laughed. "I shall be delighted," he said, "but I have a friend with me. If I might present him—"

Lord Maxwell glanced at the table, where Ouro Preto sat. "Ah! Yes! The Count of Ouro Preto. I have heard of him. Present him by all means."

Topham beckoned, and the count came over. Introductions followed. Lord Maxwell offered Topham a seat beside his own, and the ladies made room for Ouro Preto between them.

Lady Ellen, an undeveloped English girl, paused for something to say, and Miss Byrd, true to American canons, rushed into the breach.

"Isn't it lovely," she gushed, addressing Ouro Preto. "We were just admiring it all!"

Her voice and accent, like that of most Virginians, was low and cultured, but to Topham, there seemed something almost English in her locutions— something he had never noticed in the old days.

The count looked around as if he had never seen the place before.

"Heavens!" he exclaimed. "So it is!"

All laughed, Lillian most brightly of all. "One can tell that you are used to it," she mocked. "It takes strangers to note beauties—"

"Not always, Miss Byrd."

"Oh!" Lillian clapped her hands, gaily. "Good!" she nodded. "But I don't mean beauties that you can see; I mean those you can hear. Stop! Look! Listen!"

The night was clear. A near-by fountain chuckled in the moonlight; the leaves overhead stirred, rustling in the wind that moved along the tree tops. Far away, the mellow notes of a bugle sounded softly above the tinkle of the glasses. Frogs croaked in basso from the ponds. A lion in a near-by house roared, and a chorus of lesser animals answered.

"I always see in terms of sound," explained Miss Byrd.

The ice cream soda was brought. The English tasted it gingerly; the Americans hopefully. Ouro Preto gulped his and swore that it was delicious.

Lord Maxwell turned to Topham and plunged into a technical discussion of the future of the airship in war, leaving Ouro Preto to the girls—that is to say, to Lillian, for Lady Ellen, unable to keep up, contented herself with an occasional "Fancy!" coupled with glances full of admiration for the two handsome creatures by her side.

Lord Maxwell, seeing them engrossed, dropped his voice. "I'm surprised to see the count here," he observed. "He and his sister are to see the Emperor at eleven o'clock, aren't they? That's only two hours from now."

Topham started. He had been listening to his lordship, but he had been watching Lillian, wondering how he could have thought her so beautiful. The regular features, the peachy complexion, the melting blue eyes were all there, but something had gone out of them, leaving them insipid. Almost without thinking, he was comparing them with the rich coloring of the Countess Elsa.

Lord Maxwell's words startled him. He had distinctly understood Ouro Preto to say that his approaching audience was set for the next day; and he had certainly said nothing about his sister.

"Not tonight! Tomorrow," he answered. "I'm surprised that you have heard of it. I did not know the fact was generally known."

"It isn't," rejoined his lordship, drily; "and it's not for tomorrow; it's for eleven o'clock tonight. I suppose your government does not object?"

Topham stared. He remembered that Ouro Preto had also inquired as to possible objections. "Why should it," he questioned, in some bewilderment. "What has the United States to do with the creation or re-creation of a German duchy?"

Lord Maxwell glanced sharply at the American, as if wondering whether his words were as ingenuous as his tones. For a moment he hesitated; then went on.

"One never can tell," he remarked, lightly. "He is an old friend of yours, I believe?"

Topham shook his head. "Not an old friend," he corrected. "I only met him today. He seems a very pleasant fellow."

Lord Maxwell choked over the last of his soda. "I—ah—believe he is noted for his—er—affectionate nature," he murmured, when he recovered his voice. "I should like to know whether the count's friendship for you survives his meeting with the Emperor. Come and see me in a few days, won't you, Mr. Topham?"

Topham smiled. "I wish I could," he declared. "But I'm off tomorrow afternoon!"

"Ah! Is it so? I'm sorry. I should have liked to see more of you." Lord Maxwell rose. "If you girls have seen enough," he remarked, suggestively; "I think we had better be going."

With a muttered apology, Ouro Preto glanced at his watch; then leaped to his feet with an exclamation. "A most important engagement," he declared. "I must take a cab and hurry. I had no idea it was so late. Your fair kinswomen make the time fly, Lord Maxwell," he continued. "I have to thank them for a most delightful hour."

CHAPTER X

The party of four started for the embassy on foot, taking their way to where the Charlottenburg Drive cut straight through the noble Thiergarten to the Branderberger Thor and the streets of old Berlin. A few yards from the zoological garden the dazzle of the lamps died away, and only the big stars, flaring in the heavens, lighted the broad white road.

Divining the Americans' wish to exchange reminiscences, Lord Maxwell and his daughter stepped ahead, leaving the other two to follow.

The wind was rustling through the leaves; the air was damp but warm and languorous; the night seemed made for sentiment. Topham felt it and wondered what Miss Byrd expected him to say. Not knowing, he said nothing.

Miss Byrd, however, either did not feel sentimental or preferred to take another way to show it. "Well, Walter," she began, "I suppose I ought to ask about everybody and then you ought to ask about everybody and by the time we have learned all about everybody, we should be at the embassy saying good-night, without either of us knowing anything we really wanted to know. So suppose we take everybody's health for granted and talk of things we really care about."

Topham started. This girl was not the Lillian Byrd he had known. Bright, witty, and attractive she yet seemed to him almost a stranger. Perhaps, he pondered, it was because he no longer loved her, and yet—and yet—the Lillian Byrd he had known of old had possessed a very special air of refinement—one bringing memories of lavender and stately homes and dear old-fashioned ladies, while this girl seemed hardened, metallic, with a laugh that tinkled out of tune. He was silent, not knowing what to say.

Miss Byrd noticed his hesitation and attributed it instantly to the right cause.

"You think I'm changed, don't you?" she demanded. "Oh! you needn't trouble to deny it! I *am* changed. Goodness knows I've had enough to change anybody. You didn't know that I was that dreadful thing—a lady journalist— did you? I am! I'm on the New York Gazette."

"Good Heavens! You—you don't mean that you are corresponding for Risdon's paper. How in the world—"

"That's what I mean. I've been doing it for two years, and working for the Gazette is mighty hard on refinement. I can pretend still if the atmosphere is right. I haven't forgotten the old airs and graces, and I put them on at times— when I go back to Washington to see dear Aunt Polly or when—well, tonight, for instance, when I had an object. But they don't fit any more, Mr. Topham; they don't fit!"

There was a tremble in the girl's voice that suggested tears and made Topham feel acutely uncomfortable. The darkness hid his distress while he sought unreadily for some response and found none.

Nor did the girl speak again at once. In silence the two walked on through the fragrant night, the massed foliage rising on either side, a network against the sky. Here and there white statues gleamed, ghostly in the darkness, and at long intervals a street lamp cast a circle of yellow light. From off to the right came the noise of running water and the distant creak of oars or of cordage as some huge barge crept slowly along the invisible Spree. Now and then an electric car swept brilliantly along the drive.

At last the girl, with an obvious attempt at flippancy, spoke again.

"The new style comes easy to me," she said; "so easy that I guess it must be nearer my real self than the older one you used to know. I like it, though I know I ought to be ashamed of it. I look back on the old days as—as a divorceè looks back on her first honeymoon, I suppose—as a mighty pleasant time but not for her any more."

"But—but why—"

"Don't you know. Hadn't you heard about father? Really? Well, he lost his place in the War Department and then the panic came along and took his money; and then his health failed; and it was up to sister Eleanor and poor silly me to look after him and Aunt Polly. There was nobody else to do it, you see. Sister Eleanor got a job as social secretary to one of those wild western senators, but nobody seemed to want yours truly. I couldn't get a Government post because dad had been in the service so long that he had lost his residence in Kentucky, and of course nobody from the District has a chance for appointment. So at last it came down to a choice between seeing dad and Aunt Polly suffer and becoming a reportress—how I used to loathe them! Mr. McNew liked my style and sent me over to write up Europe six months ago. I've lived and dad has had some comforts and I don't think Europe has suffered much. Anyway, it's got to take its chance. I made friends with Lady Ellen in England, and she invited me to visit her in Berlin, and here I am. They like me because I am 'so American'—when I want to be."

"American! I thought you were very English tonight. You had the accent pat."

Miss Byrd laughed, a little harshly. "I always was a good mimic, wasn't I?" she asked. "Of course, it's hard for Americans to learn English; it's so much like their own language. But, my word, old chappy, I fawncy I've caught the bally idea, don't you know?"

Topham chuckled. "You surely have!" he declared. "You fooled Ouro Preto completely. He thinks you are English. Indeed, I shouldn't wonder if he thought you kin to Lord Maxwell."

"Nor I," returned Miss Byrd, drily. "You needn't bother to undeceive him, Walter. His belief may come in handy. He's from Brazil, you know, and I'm going to that out-of-the-way country, pretty soon."

"Really?"

"Really! I'm going to do the east coast and perhaps the west coast for the Gazette—write it up commercially, you know, in my racy style." The girl hesitated; then: "Oh! how I hate it all!" she burst out. "Oh! Walter! Walter! Why didn't you marry me while I was a real lady?"

Topham hesitated. He was not a ready talker, and such an opening called for quick wit or mature consideration.

"Never mind! You needn't answer! You dear good fellow! It was my fault, of course. I had ideas above a young navy officer in those days. I haven't now. But don't be afraid. I'm not fishing for a proposal. I couldn't live up to you now any more than I can live up to Aunt Polly's befo' de wah standards."

Topham looked at the girl with sadly mixed feelings. He assured himself that his feeling for her, such as it was, had vanished. Yet her seemingly cheerful renunciation was not altogether as welcome as it should have been. While he was considering his answer, Miss Byrd glanced at him out of the corner of her eye. "Who is she, Walter?" she demanded.

Topham started in good earnest. Was his secret as plainly to be read as that. "She?" he stammered.

"Of course! The one, the only she. Don't tell me you haven't met her, for I know better."

Topham found his tongue. "I never really saw 'her' till today," he said, hypocritically, with a smile and a bow. "Now that you have come—"

"Oh! nonsense! Walter! You never did know how to flirt. None of your family ever did. Their directness in love is a tradition in Virginia. You never were in love with me, really. So"—with a sudden change of tone—"so you only 'really' met her today, did you? I suppose you'll ran off with her tomorrow—as your father did. But there! I won't tease you. Are you going back to God's country soon?"

Topham drew a breath of relief. Most navy and army officers are professional squires of dames and either flirt, gossip, or drivel whenever they come into touch with a petticoat. But Topham, as Miss Byrd had suggested, did none of these. Women, especially the empty-headed ones who talked only personalities, thought him heavy. Just what Miss Byrd thought did not appear.

"Not for a year, at least, I think," he answered. "I am on my way now to Tokio. My ship leaves Brindisi day after tomorrow and I must leave tomorrow night to be sure to catch her. I came overland from Hamburg and stopped over here to see Rutile, the secretary of our embassy. He and your chief, Risdon, were both in my class at the naval academy."

Miss Byrd listened carelessly. "So you are going to Japan, are you? That means San Francisco sooner or later, of course. You'll probably be back in the United States before I am."

"How long will you stay in Berlin?"

"No time at all. I go to England tomorrow, and sail for Brazil in a month. Now that I've seen you and learned that you've found another and are her'n, there's nothing more for me to do here!" And Miss Byrd laughed, not quite genuinely, perhaps.

Topham, however, noticed nothing amiss in her tones. "It's superfluous for me to say that I'm sorry you're going," he answered; "seeing that I won't be here myself. May I call and say good-by tomorrow?"

Miss Byrd hesitated. "You probably wouldn't find me," she declared frankly. "I'm a working woman now and I've got to go and interview two or three fussy old diplomats. I don't know when I'll be at home. But I'm going to be at the American embassy some time in the afternoon, and I'll probably get a chance to say 'auf wiedersehen' there. Now, good-night! Here we are at Lord Maxwell's."

CHAPTER XI

When Topham left Miss Byrd he went back to the American embassy. The hour was late and the windows were all dark and the rooms seemed deserted, and despite Rutile's invitation for a moment Topham hesitated to climb the stairs.

Finally he stepped to the entrance, intending to ask the watchman-porter there whether the secretary had gone. To his surprise—though not so greatly so as it would have been if he had known German customs better—the door was ajar and the watchman missing; so with a shrug of his shoulders he entered and climbed the stairs.

A tap at the embassy offices brought immediate answer, and he opened the door just as Rutile came to meet him.

"Come in, old man," called the latter. "I've been sitting in the moonlight thinking something out. I often do when I've got something important on hand. Come and sit down and I'll light up and we'll have a drink."

Topham took the proffered chair, but declined the drink. "Not tonight, thank you!" he decided. "And don't light up for me. I like moonlight. Queer about the moon, though. It affects most people the other way, doesn't it?"

"Maybe! But not me! I'm rather excitable, you know. Liable to get worked up over things and to exaggerate their importance. When I suspect I'm doing that, I sit down in the moonlight—if there's a moon handy—and in the stillness—if stillness is to be had—and think it all over. That's what I've been doing tonight."

"And did it soothe you?"

Rutile shook his head, doubtfully. "I'm not certain," he admitted. "You navy people have the best of it, after all. You haven't got to agitate your supposed brains. All you've got to do is to fight, and if you get a chance to distinguish yourself the whole country knows it and the Sunday newspapers call you heroes and clamor for your promotion. We diplomats, on the other hand, are valuable in the inverse ratio that we make it known."

"Yes?" remarked Topham, languidly.

"Yes! Of course!" returned Rutile, impatiently. "We diplomats are the real defenders of the peace. Suppose we had a war! All you fellows could do would be to whip the enemy and if you did it you would get medals and prize money and things. But I've prevented at least one war and nobody knows anything about it except the last administration at Washington and if there's any deader tomb for a man's achievements than the last administration, I don't know where it is—unless it's the administration before the last."

Topham fidgeted. He was not very apt at speech. "What war did you prevent?" he asked, at last, seeing that Rutile expected him to say something.

"Oh! None of any special consequence," returned the other sarcastically, "Just a little bit of a war—one between Germany and the United States."

"You're joking, aren't you?"

"Never less so. His Majesty Wilhelm was working to grab southern Brazil two or three years ago and I checkmated him; knocked his plans sky-high. If I hadn't we'd have had to fight him or abandon the Monroe Doctrine. And just because I did it so quietly nobody knew anything about it, bright young men like you want to know whether I am serious; even the Ambassador has his doubts on the subject."

Topham was not listening. Rutile's mention of Brazil had given him the opening he desired.

"That reminds me," he said, awkwardly, "What do you think of Count Ouro Preto and his sister? Risdon was speaking of them this morning, you know. They're Brazilians, aren't they?"

Rutile swallowed. It is not altogether pleasant to be checked so abruptly when talking about one's self. Then he laughed.

"You're the directest ever!" he remarked. "Why didn't you tell me you wanted to know about the Countess Elsa, and save me telling you a lot of stuff you didn't listen to? I suppose you have found out that it was she who crossed with you?"

Topham stared. "Yes!" he said. "Risdon pointed her out on the street this morning and I recognized her. How did you guess?"

"Oh! Easily! Her name really is Elsa Ferreira, you know. The title is very new—one of Dom Pedro's creations just before he was turned out by the republic. So she's been to New York! She's been missing from here for about three weeks, and people have been wondering where she was."

"Tell me something about her."

Rutile threw up his hands. "I haven't time to do justice to the subject," he declared. "She came to Berlin about six months ago, and promptly got the whole hoch wohlgebornen bunch at her feet, men and women too. She's beautiful, but it isn't altogether her looks, you know; it's her amazing knowledge of men and things. They say she hired out once as a chambermaid and at another time worked in a factory here. They also say that she was the masked unknown who caused such a sensation by dancing as Salome for charity in the most outrageous costume that ever—"

"I don't believe it!" Topham's face was flushed and his eyes glittered.

Rutile studied him curiously. The dispatches Topham had brought had been devoted wholly to the Count and Countess del Ouro Preto. The navy officer did not know this, of course, but Rutile felt very sure that he believed the two were behind the efforts that had been made to rob him of them. Knowing the fascinations of the countess, the secretary had little hesitation in guessing that Topham had fallen a victim to them. He wanted to warn him, but scarcely knew how to begin. After all, Topham was going away in twenty-four hours, and the first canon of friendship is "don't butt in."

So he changed the subject. "Hope you enjoyed yourself tonight," he observed.

"Finely! I went to your Thiergarten and met several people I knew—Lord Maxwell, the British Ambassador, and young Ferreira—the Count del Ouro Preto, I should say—and—"

"Ouro Preto!" Rutile was startled. "What did he want?"

Topham considered. "Nothing!" he answered. "He was full of his coming audience with the emperor and—"

"Audience with the emperor!" Rutile was on his feet. "What do you mean? Has Ouro Preto seen the emperor?"

Topham drew out his watch and consulted it. "Well!" he said. "It's now 12:45, so I may safely say that he has. He was to be received at eleven o'clock tonight."

"You're sure?"

"Well! not entirely! Ouro Preto himself said the appointment was for ten o'clock tomorrow, but Lord Maxwell said it was for eleven tonight, and I suspect that Ouro Preto was mistaken."

Rutile sat down again, slowly. "So do I," he replied, drily. "But what I most want to know is, why did he tell you about it?"

Topham laughed. "Oh! he was too full of it to keep still. Pure spontaneousness!"

"Spontaneous fiddlesticks! What did *you* say? What did he ask you?"

"Why! I don't know! Nothing important. Let's see. I believe he said he feared somebody might oppose the restoration of the dukedom, and that he was afraid to speak to most people about it, but that he could talk to me because of course the United States had no interest—"

"Oh!"

"Eh? Yes! I told him of course we hadn't. Queer, though! Lord Maxwell asked me later almost the same thing. Wanted to know whether the United States objected to the Kaiser giving Ouro Preto his toy? As if the United States had any interest in petty German dukedoms!"

Rutile threw up his hands. "Lord! Lord!" he cried. "I suppose you told Maxwell that?" he queried.

"Of course. What the devil is the matter with you, Rutile?"

For an instant the secretary stared at the navy officer, without speaking. "Look here, Topham," he said at last. "I want to know whether you are the guileless child I have always supposed you to be, or whether you are so infernally deep that even I can't fathom you. Confound you, man, you've had me guessing ever since you got here. You—"

Abruptly the secretary broke off and leaned forward. "What's that?" he questioned, whisperingly.

The night was very still. Traffic in the street outside had almost ceased—for the moment had ceased altogether. Not even a footfall sounded. But from somewhere close at hand there came a slight grating sound.

"Sounds like somebody sawing," muttered Topham. "What—

"Sshh!" A grin of perfect comprehension came over Rutile's face. "Gently!" he whispered. "Somebody's trying to break into the embassy's rooms. And I think I can guess who it is. But we'll give him the surprise of his life. Come."

He arose and tiptoed to the door of the adjoining room, and opened it cautiously. Like the one in which the two had sat, this room was dark except for the brilliant moonlight that streamed in at the uncurtained windows. It was empty, but the sound of the sawing was much more distinct. Evidently the would-be intruder was close at hand.

Silently Rutile approached the door that gave upon the corridor without and pointed to the lock. Something was moving in and out just above it, and in a moment Topham distinguished the blade of a saw working through the woodwork. Four augur holes had been bored at the corners of an imaginary square, and some one was slowly joining them, with the evident intention of making an opening through which he might slip his arm and shoot back the bolts.

Rutile looked at Topham with twinkling eyes. With a gesture for silence he tiptoed to a closet and with infinite caution took out a light but strong rope.

This he handed to Topham. "You're a sailor," he said under his breath. "Make a dip noose."

With an instant understanding of what he proposed, Topham hastily knotted the line, and returned it to the secretary. The latter stepped close to the door, where the saw had almost completed its work, and stood waiting.

Soon the saw was drawn back, a finger appeared through the augur hole, closed around the edge of the square and exerted a gentle pressure. With scarcely a sound the wood yielded, and the piece was drawn gently out.

With baited breath the two men waited. Evidently those without were listening. Then an arm came through the hole and a hand began to feel for the key. Instantly Rutile slipped his rope around the wrist, drew it tight, and threw himself back on the rope.

A startled exclamation came from the outside, and then the prisoned man began a desperate though silent struggle for liberty. But he was at a terrible disadvantage. Inch by inch, his arm was drawn until his body was fast against the door; then there was a sudden yielding. "My God," cried a voice. "Stop! You're killing me. I surrender. I'll tell everything. I'll— Stop! Stop! Don't strike! I'll keep faith. I'll—" The words ended with a thick choking hiccough.

"Hold this, Topham," ordered Rutile, passing over the rope. "I'll ring for the police."

He pressed the burglar alarm on the wall, lighted the gas and was back at the door. "Now we'll see what we've caught," he declared, turning the key in the lock.

The door swung open and, with the relaxing of the rope, a man's body pitched down upon the threshold and lay there, his upturned face ghastly in the glare of the gas jets. From his breast projected the handle of a dagger, whose blade had been driven in to the hilt, and, and across the white bosom of his shirt a crimson stain was widening. It needed no second glance to see that he was dead.

Rutile studied the dark face. "Looks like a Spaniard or a Spanish-American," he decided. "Just about what I would have expected. But I never saw him before!"

Topham said nothing. His brain was whirling. For he, at least, had seen the man's face before. It was that of the Spanish-American who had given him the drugged cigarette—of the man whom he had seen only a few hours before coming down the steps of the building that housed the Countess Elsa.

CHAPTER XII

The attempted burglary at the American Embassy made quite a stir, not only in Berlin but in America. That it did not make a greater one was due to the fact that no one except Rutile and Topham suspected that it was anything more than the simple attempt at burglary that it seemed; and both Rutile and Topham had their own reasons for concealing their suspicions.

The attempt was therefore ascribed simply to a desire for plunder; that it might have political significance was not even publicly suggested. So far as Rutile knew, Risdon was the only one to smell even the smallest rat; and Risdon, having absolutely no information concerning the letter Topham had brought, knew nothing that connected Ouro Preto with the incident. He therefore found so little on which to base a story, that he cabled only a vague surmise that nobody paid any attention to.

But despite the fact that few people suspected any particular mystery in the motive, everybody took a very great interest in the crime. The dead man was plainly not a common thief. His clothing was good and his person showed evidences of refinement. He was unknown to the police, and was therefore presumably not a member of the ordinary criminal classes. Very obviously, too, he had been murdered by his companion to do away with any chance that he might betray that companion's identity.

Few criminals go so far as to murder a "pal" under such circumstances, and from this it was argued that the accomplice must be a man who had much more than the ordinary at stake. In other words, it seemed very probable that he was a Raffles in real life. Naturally, such a suggestion was nuts to the newspaper men and they used it to the full.

Topham and Rutile shrank from discussing the subject with each other, and from resuming the broken-off conversation of the night before. It was easy enough to avoid further talk at first. The police had come promptly and had done what they had to do with neatness and dispatch. But it all took time and when it was over the dawn was at hand and the two young men went off to their beds, glad of the excuse to postpone explanations.

But Topham could not stay away from the Embassy all the next day. He was leaving in the afternoon and to absent himself would have been more significant than anything he could say. So about noon he went to the embassy, uncertain just what he would say but resolved not to shirk any question that might rightfully be asked of him.

As he approached the door he saw Caesar standing on the steps staring around him with wildly rolling eyeballs. Evidently he was looking for someone, but as his eyes passed over Topham without pausing, the latter did not guess that he himself was the object of the darkey's solicitude.

Only when he was quite near he spoke. "Well, Caesar!" he questioned, "Can't you find him?"

"Find who?" The negro whirled round. "Fore Gord, Massa Topham! Whar you come from. If I ain't been a-lookin' an' a-lookin foh you! Massa Rutile's mighty anxious to see you, suh. Please to walk up to his room, suh. Please, suh!"

Topham ascended the stairs slowly and pushed open the door of the secretary's office.

Rutile was bending over a huge atlas, but when the navy officer entered he pushed it aside. "Hello! Topham," he called. "I was getting anxious about you. Your train goes pretty soon, doesn't it?"

Topham nodded. "In an hour or so," he answered, quietly.

"I thought as much. Well! We haven't much time to waste and I will come right to the point. I want you to believe that what I am going to say I say as a representative of the United States to an officer of the United States Navy. I don't want to pry into your affairs. But I do want all the information I can get about the Count of Ouro Preto and his sister—No! let me go on— Risdon told me of your agitation on meeting the countess on the street yesterday. I know myself that you are interested in her. I know, too, that Ouro Preto was trying to pump you last night. We both know more about your trip across the ocean than we perhaps care to say. We both suspect much about that so-called burglary. But the point of it all is that the United States is greatly interested in this Ouro Preto matter—in anything that concerns Germany and Brazil for that matter. I have seen Lord Maxwell. He is positive that Ouro Preto saw the emperor last night and he believes that the Kaiser has offered to recognize his claims to that dukedom on conditions. What these conditions are I don't know, and it may be important that I should. You are leaving for Japan and will be out of the way later. Now, can't you tell me anything that would throw light on the matter?"

"On the question of the dukedom?" he asked. "Not a thing. Absolutely nothing!"

Rutile hesitated. "I don't want to offend you, old man," he burst out. "But I must go on. There is a big game afoot, and the Ouro Preto may well wish to keep in touch with a navy officer. The countess Elsa may be fooling you and—"

"Stop!" Topham leaned forward. "I don't misunderstand you, Rutile, my friend," he said. "You are quite right from your point of view, and I will tell you all I may. First, though, I must tell you that today I asked the Countess Elsa to marry me—"

"Marry you!" Rutile sprang to his feet.

"To marry me," reiterated the navy man, steadily, "and she accepted me—provisionally. I am to go away now and come for her in a year. During the year, I am neither to see her nor write to her. She said that—that my honor was at stake. I did not know what she meant. Her words, however, are significant. They may confirm your suspicions—whatever these are. More, I recognized the man who was murdered last night outside that door yonder."

"You did!"

"Yes! He came over on the steamer with me. I smoked a cigarette he had given me just before I was taken ill. I saw him at the hotel of the countess yesterday. I do not doubt that he and the count and perhaps the countess have tried to get those papers from me."

"And yet—"

"And yet I love her and hope to marry her. That she and her friends tried to rob me is of no importance. It's high politics. Murder is different, but she, of course, had no hand in that and probably none in the burglary. That would be Ouro Preto's part."

Rutile nodded. "Very probably," he agreed.

"I tell you this," Topham went on, "because I am an officer of the United States, sworn to its service. No navy officer has any right to hold confidential secrets that may be inimical to his country. The countess herself would be the first to say so. I do not feel called upon to take my knowledge to the police, but my country is certainly entitled to it. Of course you are at liberty to use it in any way the interests of the United States may demand."

"Of course," Rutile gasped. Topham's words seemed to have dumbfounded him. He had intended to denounce the Ouro Pretos—to show Topham the instructions he had received concerning them and warn him against them. But the navy officer's amazing declaration upset his plans. Topham knew everything of importance—and did not care. Very well! Let him dream away his year of probation; he would be far out of reach away off there in Japan, and at the end of that time the countess could be relied on to cast him over.

"Have—have you seen the countess today?" he questioned. "Does she know that—"

Topham's face flushed. "The countess told me yesterday that she was leaving Berlin at once," he said, coldly. "So I was not surprised to find her gone when

I went to her hotel this morning." He rose. "That is absolutely all I know," he finished. "Now I must be off."

"Not just yet." Rutile flung out his hand impulsively. "Not until I have thanked you, old man. I know how hard it is for you to tell me all this, and I appreciate your doing it. And I want to congratulate you. The countess is the most beautiful and brilliant woman I ever knew. You will find yourself much envied when the news is known."

Topham took the hand the other extended. "Thank you, old fellow," he murmured.

"And," went on the secretary, banteringly, "if I ever suggested that you were slow, I want to take it all back. You're the swiftest ever. To stop over in Berlin two days and carry off the biggest prize in the matrimonial market sure does break the record!"

Topham grinned. "It was rather quick," he admitted. "It's a way we Tophams have." Then he glanced at the clock above the desk. "My hour's up," he exclaimed. "Good-by, Rutile. Tell Risdon I'm sorry not to have seen him again. Good-by."

When he was gone Rutile stood for a moment gazing out of the window. Then he swore aloud. "It's a damned shame," he muttered. "Topham's the most open-hearted fellow I ever knew, the very sort to take a woman's word for gospel. Great Scott, how does she do it?" He took a turn or two up and down the room. "After all, though," he went on, thinking aloud. "It isn't how she does it. It's why does she want to do it? What use can Topham be to her in Japan? What possible use can he be to her?"

It never occurred to the secretary that the countess might be in earnest.

CHAPTER XIII

"Are you really going?"

"Really." Miss Byrd nodded. "Yes! I'm off tonight. My stay in Berlin has been delightful, largely because you have made it so, Mr. Rutile, but I hate to go. But business is business; and this stone doesn't gather any moss unless she keeps on rolling. So—" she paused.

She was pale and her delicate features seemed a trifle pinched; her lips had not their usual redness. But her tones were brisk and her manner gay.

Rutile studied her consideringly. His naturally impulsive nature had been modified by training and was held in bond by his will.

"I too have found your stay delightful," he said slowly. "I only wish I could have made it sufficiently pleasant to you to cause you to stay longer in spite of the loss of moss. When shall we meet again?"

Miss Byrd looked him frankly in the eyes; it suddenly occurred to Rutile that he had not realized their depth and color. "Who knows?" she questioned, lightly. "If I lose my job, I may have to go back to Washington; and all diplomats have to go there sooner or later to look after their jobs. So we may meet again in Washington—if it is written that we are to meet at all."

Rutile nodded. "If it isn't, it shall be," he declared. "And I don't think it will be in Washington, either; I've got a hunch that we are to—well, see exciting times together. Didn't you ever feel like that about anybody?"

"Often!" Miss Byrd giggled. "I called this morning on the high well-geborn field marshal Sweinpeltz and I felt that way the minute I saw him. And it came true within ten seconds. My! You should have heard him swear."

"Swear?"

"Well, 'Mein Gott' is swearing, isn't it? He said that three times the first question I asked him. Seriously, though, Mr. Rutile, I hope I shall see you again. Just now, I'm bound for Brazil, as you know. Any little commission I can execute for you in Buenos Ayres or Pernambuco or anywhere?"

Rutile moved a little restlessly in his chair. His eyes avoided those of the girl. "Well, yes!" he said. "There is something, but I hardly know how to ask you. It is a little—awkward."

Miss Byrd shrugged her shoulders. "Why should it be?" she asked, "You have thought it? If you have thought it of me, it must be perfectly proper. Therefore, put it into words just as you thought it? I permit you."

"Thank you! I'll take you at your word."

Rutile considered for a moment. Clearly he was marshalling his ideas. Miss Byrd's newspaper training, brief as it had been, had taught her the advisability of letting her victims have all the rope they wanted. Rutile was not a victim, but the principle was the same. So she waited in silence.

"There are two young Brazilians here," he began at last, "Who came to Berlin some weeks ago on a peculiar errand. They are the Count of Ouro Preto and his sister. Perhaps you know of them?"

Miss Byrd nodded. "Certainly I do. I wrote them up in my best style a week ago. Haughty grand duke. Fascinating ballet girl. Beautiful daughter. Dashing piratical adventurer. Mad love. Flight. Adventurer becomes governor and accumulates enormous wealth. Children seek rehabilitation of ballet girl. Prove that she was descended from Noah's ark. Haughty Wilhelm refuses even to see 'em. America demands in thunder tones why he doesn't grant her panatella children their rights. Hip! Hip! Hurrah! Anything the matter with that?"

"Nothing!" Rutile shrugged his shoulders slightly, but laughed admiringly as he did so. "Nothing much, that is, only the essential detail that Wilhelm has seen them and seems to have promised to give them what they ask."

"Really?" Miss Byrd's eyes danced. "Really? That's fine! May I use it? My story isn't printed yet and I can change it by cable."

"You may say he has seen them and is considering the matter if you like, but I wouldn't say outright that he has granted their request. I don't know that he has. If he has it was probably on conditions. What I want to know is what those conditions were."

The girl's expression changed instantly. She drew her breath quickly. Rutile's tones hinted a story, and a "story" had come to be the great thing in her life as it is in every newspaper writer's.

"*You* want to know?" she echoed. "Officially or not officially? As United States representative or as an individual?"

"Both! Brazil has a large German population; and any dealings between the Kaiser and Brazilians are of interest to the United States. It's a pretty big thing Ouro Preto has asked, and if the Kaiser does it, the United States would like to know why. That's official! But there's the unofficial side of it. I have a friend who is here for a day or two—a navy officer named Topham."

"Oh!" Miss Byrd started. "I know him," she added, after an instant's hesitation.

"Really?" Very plainly Rutile was taken aback. He took a moment to consider. "If I had known that you knew him," he went on, at last, "I think

I should not have broached the subject; and yet, after all, I think I am justified. I should not be a real friend if I did not try to help him—and he needs help. You will understand, of course, that what I am going to say is confidential."

"Certainly."

"Topham got here yesterday morning. It seems that he crossed from New York with the countess, who had slipped away from Berlin without anyone being the wiser. Topham left her at Hamburg. But yesterday morning he saw her on the street, and was much stirred up. In the afternoon he called on her. Now, not an hour ago, just before he started for his train, he tells me that she has promised to marry him. Isn't it the most preposterous—"

"Not at all! Not at all! It's splendid! Splendid! Just the sort of thing Walter Topham would do. It's traditional with his family. Everybody in Virginia knows what the Tophams are. They have run off with their wives—or with other men's—for three hundred years. They are slow and careful in most things, but when they fall in love—really in love—they sweep everything before them. Oh! I know them! I told Walter last night that I knew he was in love."

"But the countess!"

"We—ll!" Miss Byrd raised her eyebrows and flashed an amused glance at the secretary. "Well! Why not?" she questioned. "A girl, countess or not, doesn't often get a chance at a man like Walter, and I guess she's not very conventional herself, is she? With her ancestry—"

"But it's not possible! She's fooling him—playing with him. It's all bound up in some way with this dukedom business. She's using him—though for the life of me, I can't see how. Perhaps I could guess if I knew the Kaiser's conditions; and if I did know them I might save him. That's my unofficial reason for wanting to know. If you are a friend of Topham's you will help me."

"Of course! But I'll help you more because you ask me to, for I believe the engagement is bona fide, preposterous as it may seem. What do you want me to do?"

Rutile leaned back in his chair. "That depends!" he answered. "Perhaps nothing at all. But when you get to Brazil find out all you can about the Ouro Pretos. They're very prominent people. Perhaps the Kaiser's conditions may be known down there before they are up here. There may be a big newspaper story in it, but if there is I rely on you to keep Topham's name out. Again, there may be nothing. But if you'll keep me informed of anything that may develop, whether you print it or not, you may do a service to Topham and also to the United States. Will you do it?"

"Will I? Of course I will."

CHAPTER XIV

"Say, Topham! I'm mighty glad to see you." Stites, secretary of legation in Tokio, lifted his wine glass and leaned across the spotless cloth. "Mighty glad to see you. A glass of wine with you, old man."

Topham lifted his glass and smiled. "Thank you," he answered. "It makes a fellow feel good to be welcomed like this. You people have been mighty good to me."

"Oh! Well!" Stites laughed. "We'll show you the other side of it tomorrow."

The two young men sat at a little round table at the English Hotel where nightly the foreigners and the fashionable world of Tokio dined and criticized each other's clothes. Around them were men and women of all types— Germans, English, a few Americans, fewer French, many Japanese, some in native dress and others looking strangely awkward in European garments. Little dark waiters slipped swiftly, though not hurriedly, through the throng. The hum of conversation, punctuated by the click of ice on the rims of delicate glasses rose above the thrumming of the quaint oriental music. The night was heavy with the perfume of lilies. Far away, through the broad windows, across the roofs of the city, the bay gleamed silvery in the moonlight.

Topham took it all in. "It's beautiful," he said. "Beautiful! I've never been to Japan before and it—well, it's overpowering."

"Of course! Everything is, in this country. We've got maids at the embassy— the custom of the country, my boy—that are dreams of loveliness. Madame l'Ambassadrice objected and to please her I tried to get ugly ones. Nothing doing, my boy. There aren't any in Japan—except those that wear Melican man's clothes."

Topham smiled. "I like it," he said.

"Oh! Do you, indeed! Naturally you would. All sailors do. But look out, old man. Times aren't what they used to be. Don't trust the old romances on Japan or you'll get into trouble."

"I won't." Topham stared around him. All about were interesting-looking men and pretty women. "Who's that?" he asked. "The tall man at the table to your right?"

"That's Cosdon, the British naval attaché! There's the Spanish attaché just beyond. Most of the attachés dine here. I'll introduce you to a bunch of them after a while. You'll be the whole works at our shop, you know. We haven't had any sort of attaché, navy or army, for six months. And we've needed 'em; needed 'em like the devil."

"Why?"

"Why what? Why did we need them? Well, you can't play chess without pawns. You fellows are the pawns. We diplomats can't play spy, you know; but you navy and army men are licensed."

Topham raised his eyebrows. "Why not use the natives?" he asked; "or are they too patriotic?"

"Patriotic nothing! That's all bunkum just like the jiu jitsu. The Japs are no better than any other nation and I guess they're a little worse. They've got cowards and traitors just like other people—maybe more so. But you can't trust traitors, you know; they won't stay hitched. Besides, we need skilled men. The Chief has been cabling to Washington for attachés for six months, but the cotillions didn't seem willing to spare anybody until you came. And they sent you in the end by the longest way round."

Topham looked his sympathy. It had been three months since he had left Berlin. The Nevada, which he had joined at Brindisi, had dawdled along via Port Said, Aden, and Singapore and had reached Manila just too late to enable him to catch the swift, direct passenger steamer for Japan and compelling him to take a much slower and roundabout boat.

"I could have come quicker," he admitted. "But the Nevada needed a watch officer, and—"

"And so you spent three months in coming by water instead of ten days coming by Siberian railway. And all the while the need for you here was increasing. I understand you speak Japanese, Topham."

"A little!"

"Only a little?" The secretary was disappointed. "That's bad—unless it's only your beastly polite way of disdaining knowledge. Well! you've got your work cut out for you here! The Japs mean to fight us, and we have been grossly negligent in preparing for them. We haven't even informed ourselves as to the extent of their preparations. The Chief has done what he could, but it hasn't been much."

Topham leaned back and let his eyes rove over the expanse of city and bay beneath the windows. No scene could be more peaceful. War seemed to him far-off and impossible.

"You really think they mean to fight?" he questioned. His tones expressed doubt, though much less than he felt.

"Of course! Of course! No doubt at all! They want to fight and they will fight. The only question is as to when they'll fight. Japan means to be the England of the Pacific, and she means to dominate China, including Corea and

Manchuria. The open door—Bah! No Japanese intends to allow it a moment longer than he must. Oh! they'll fight! And they're getting ready to fight now."

Topham listened respectfully. Listening was Topham's long suit. But he did not for an instant believe.

"Is there anything new," he asked. "Things seemed quiet enough in Manila. Of course, I was there for only a day and hadn't much time to pick up details. There was something in one of the papers about some trouble in San Francisco, I believe; but—"

"That's the opening. A sort of gambit, you know. The Japs there claim they have a treaty right to send grown Japanese men to study in the public schools with white boys and girls—girls, you understand. It's intolerable, of course! But they are using it as a pretext to stir up bad blood. They're cunning. They are trying to make capital for themselves in Europe and particularly in England. Blood is thicker than water and they'll have to have a mighty good excuse for war with the United States if they want England's sympathy. And what's more," the secretary leaned forward, "I have reason to believe that they are dickering with Germany!"

Topham started and picked up his glass hastily, to mask his movement. Since he had met the Countess Elsa, any mention of Germany made his pulses stir.

"Natural enough, isn't it?" he questioned. "Of course Japan would want to be on good terms with Germany. Probably she would like to be on terms with France, too; and perhaps even with Russia. But why should that mean anything against the United States. Frankly, Stites, I'm from Missouri on the Japanese question. You'll have to show me!"

"Events will do that all right," rejoined the other, a trifle grimly. "But, with Germany, it's scarcely a question. Ever since that woman got here—"

"What woman?"

"The smartest, prettiest woman I ever knew and that's saying something. Say, Topham, did you ever play stud-poker?"

"Well, I've *heard* of it," admitted the officer, grinning.

"Oh! Have you? Well! you know how it's played? The dealer deals one card around face down, and everybody looks at it secretly. Then he deals around again and again, card by card, all face up, until each man has a full poker hand. After each round, you bet what you like. All the cards in all the hands except one are exposed. It's the one secret card that makes the doubt in the game. Only one card, and yet it makes the game more exciting than if all five were hidden. Well! diplomacy is much like that—especially diplomacy as this woman plays it. She has shown all her cards except one—what Germany is to get out of it all. A mighty clever woman, Topham, and as pretty as she is clever."

"Who is she?"

"Well, now, who knows. She calls herself—" the secretary broke off and craned his neck, trying to make out more clearly the identity of a little group of people who had just entered the dining-room. "She usually comes here to dine," he went on, slowly, "And maybe—yes! There she is. She's the lady approaching—the one in grey. She calls herself the Countess Elsa del Ouro Preto. Sounds Spanish, but she is really German as they make 'em."

Topham never knew how he got to his feet. There was a roaring in his ears and the lights danced around him. Only one thing held steady—the splendid eyes of the Countess Elsa.

She was coming toward him. Her tiny jewelled slippers made no sound on the mats that covered the floor, but her silken robes swished as she moved. In the aureole of her hair trembled a single diamond; a belt of rubies clasped her waist. Ah! How beautiful she was. How she fitted into the scheme of things in this bizarre eastern world! Topham's glass shattered in his hand and the pieces tinkled on the floor as he looked.

Then she saw him. For an instant the traitor blood ebbed to her heart, leaving her face whiter than man had ever seen it before. Then it rushed back in a crimson tide, burning. But she walked on. Her eyes held Topham's for a second; then wandered indifferently past. Carelessly she turned to the huge blonde German who walked by her side—a man with the broad ribbon of the Black Eagle across his breast—and made some laughing remark. Indifferently, without sign of recognition, she passed—passed to where an obsequious waiter held a chair ready.

Topham's legs gave way under him. It needed not the protests of the horror-stricken secretary to drag him down into his chair.

"For God's sake, man! Careful! Everybody is watching you! Do you know her?"

Topham shook his head slowly. "I thought I did," he muttered. "But—I do not."

CHAPTER XV

At last it was over. The intolerable evening had dragged itself to an end. Topham had laughed and joked and made merry far beyond his custom or his nature, trying to dull the sting at his heart and to conceal from Stites and his companions the misery that oppressed him. He had met scores of men and women; had received dozens of informal invitations from the men; and had laid the foundations of many friendships.

But all the while he was longing to be alone—to get time to think what was portended by this amazing apparition of the woman he loved. At last, when the throng had thinned; when the last of his new-made friends had nodded himself away; when even Stites had left him with a warning that on the morrow he would "show him some stunts", Topham wandered to the edge of the broad terrace in front of the hotel and sat down to think.

The night was redolent of perfume. The gardens—the wonderful Japanese gardens where all sense of distance is lost and one wanders through miles of woodland, climbs mountains, and crosses lakes, all in the space of a few yards—stretched around him, limitless and mysterious. No moon shone, but the planets globed themselves in the star-dusted heavens and cast a pale radiance over meadow and wood. A soft night wind, warm and caressing, whispered of the age-old mystery of the east. From far away rose the murmur of the city stirring in its invisible homes. The night birds called from the bushes.

Insensibly the calm stole on Topham's senses, and his whirling thoughts composed themselves. The Countess had reached Tokio before him; from what Stites said she had been there for several weeks at least; most likely she had left Berlin almost as soon as he had, and had come by way of Russia and Port Arthur.

Why was she there? Had she come because of him or for some reason of her own? Had she known that he was under orders for Tokio before she met him in Berlin and could her kindness have concealed some plan to use him— him a naval officer in the United States service? Or was she really ignorant that he was bound for the east. He could not remember having told her, and she might very well not have known his destination—might have understood him to be permanently attached to the Nevada. Remembering what she had said of a task that she was working out, he could not but think that her presence in Japan had to do with that task.

If she were on an errand of her own, what was it? He remembered that Rutile had believed that the Kaiser would set conditions for the restoration of the lost duchy; probably the countess was trying to fulfill these conditions.

But what were the Kaiser's conditions. Shrink as he might from questioning the acts of the woman he loved, he could not forget the role that Stites had ascribed to her. Putting beside this her own assertions that association with her spelled peril to his honor the obvious explanation was that she was engaged in some proceeding inimical to his country—some conspiracy that it was his duty as an officer of the United States to discover and to crush.

He set himself to studying out the possible objects of a possible conspiracy. Clearly it involved Japan. But how? The obvious explanation was that it had to do with trade—the open door—Manchuria—China; but somehow Topham doubted whether the obvious explanation were the true one. He remembered Stites's assertion that Japan was preparing for war with the United States. But what had Germany to do in such a war, even if it should be contemplated? What could she possibly gain that would balance even the loss that would result from the disturbance of trade? The Kaiser had been angry when the United States seized the Philippines years before, but having held his wrath then, how could he hope to profit by it now? If Japan got the better of the struggle, the spoils would go to her and not to Germany. On its face, a Japanese-German war conspiracy against the United States was preposterous.

Yet he could not doubt that Germany was in some way for some reason involved. But how? But how? Mortified self pride played no part in Topham's reflections. Although the Countess had "cut" him in the dining-room, decidedly, unmistakably, the fact had almost ceased to trouble him. She might have very good reasons for not desiring to seem to know him at that moment; he was content to wait for an explanation. Besides, he had more important things to think about.

A clatter of clogs on the stones of the terrace and a rustling of garments aroused him and he looked around to find a Japanese maid bowing profoundly in the starlight just behind his right shoulder.

"Hello!" he exclaimed, startled. "What want?"

The girl closed her fan with a clash just as he had seen her sisters do it many a time on the stage in America.

"Ees thees the honorable Meester Topham?" she asked in a high harsh voice.

Topham nodded. "Yes!" he said, briefly. "You look for me, eh?" he questioned, inanely.

"He-e-e-sh!" The girl giggled. It struck Topham that there was something artificial about that giggle. It sounded stagy. Besides there was nothing for the girl to laugh at—unless it were himself. He moved uncomfortably.

"The honorable meester want to see honorable lady?"

"Ah!" Topham drew in his breath sharply. So this was it!

"Yes! Yes!" he answered, eagerly. "You come from her? Where is she?

"You love—honorable lady?" squeaked the girl.

Topham was past caution now. "More than life," he cried. "Take me to her! Quick!"

The girl bowed humbly. "Honorable gentleman follow," she commanded and turned away down a white path that led into the depths of the garden.

Topham followed eagerly. All around him the grasses rustled in the night breeze. The crossed branches of the trees rubbed softly against each other. The scent of the water lilies grew sweeter.

So she brought him to the margin of a tiny lake set in the midst of turf that sank like velvet beneath his feet. There beside a carved statue of an unknown god she paused, and he paused, too, waiting for he knew not what.

Tiny wavelets broke on the white pebbles. The lily pads rocked on them, rising and sinking, shimmering white in the starlight. Suddenly the girl stood up, rising for the first time to her full height.

"Walter!" she cried. "Walter! Walter!"

Topham did not speak. He could not. But he held out his arms and drew her to his heart. "Elsa!" he murmured, after a while, and again, "Elsa! Elsa!"

She stirred in his arms. "I love you! I love you!" she murmured. "Ah! Do you know that I nearly fainted when you faced me there tonight! Cruel! Cruel! Not to give me warning!"

Topham drew her closer. "I did not know!" he breathed. "I did not know. And yet how could I not know?"

Gently the countess freed herself. "Sit down," she ordered. "Here! Where I can touch you, but not where I can look into your eyes. I—I could not trust myself else. Do you know dear, you have wonderful eyes."

Topham laughed. "I! Nonsense! You mean that *you* have!"

"No! I mean you have. There is enchantment in them, if you like. How else could a single glance from them across a crowded street bring me—me— Elsa de Ouro Preto—to your feet. My face burns when I think how I fell into your arms—and yet I would not have it otherwise. Dios! Walter! What have you done to me?"

"Not more than you have done to me—"

"Hush! There is no time. I shall be missed and then—"

"Missed. Who—"

"Now! Now! Now! No one you need trouble your head about. But let me talk. I am here on a political mission—you must have guessed that. I cannot let you become involved in it. There are reasons—you will not ask me for them—but there are good reasons why you must not be suspected of any association with me or my work."

Topham's eyes grew troubled. "Tell me one thing," he begged. "Tell me—"

"No! No! I can tell you nothing. I will not lie to you and I can not tell you the truth. You may suspect what you please. It is your right. But you may not ask me anything. It would do no good and might do much harm. That is why I pretended not to know you in the dining-room tonight. That is why I have slipped out to you in this guise. I could not come in any other. It is best that no one should know that you know me!"

"May I not meet you? May I not be presented? May I not—"

The countess's breath came faster. "No! No!" she gasped. "No! No! I could not bear it. Besides there will be no chance. I leave tomorrow."

The blood flowed back to Topham's heart. Unconsciously his grasp upon the girl tightened until she could have screamed from very pain. "Tomorrow!" he muttered. "Tomorrow! Tomorrow!"

"I must." The woman was sobbing. "I must! Duty calls. I have to leave for America—for Washington—for your own country, where I must work out my task. Where it will lead—what its consequences will be—God knows! I would give it up if I could, but I am bound by a promise to the dead. Dead lips can not give back the spoken word and I must go on. Ah!"—she turned and flung her arms fiercely around the man—"Ah! I am mad!—insane! But I love you! I love you!"

Over the shadowy pool the night mist hung, wavering in the starlight. A distant cataract—or was it a near-by rill—thundered away off in the night. The stones and grass were wet with dew. Topham saw them sparkling iridescent on the black island that rose in the middle of the lake.

Suddenly the woman sprang up. "They will miss me," she cried. "I must go. There—there is danger."

"Do not go. Not yet. Stay a little—only a little. It is so long—so long—"

"I must! I—I cannot see. There is a mist over my eyes—"

"It is a cloud! No, it your hair! No! it is my lips—"

CHAPTER XVI

After Lillian Byrd and Topham had left Berlin, their relative importance in Rutile's eyes underwent a gradual change. Anxious at first to hear from Miss Byrd chiefly because he hoped she might be able to discover something that might aid him to rescue his friend from what he felt sure was a dangerous entanglement, he soon became anxious to hear from her for her own sake. Therefore, he eagerly welcomed the letters she wrote him even before she left for Brazil, and he spent much time and used up much midnight oil in preparing answers.

Both the Ouro Pretos had left Berlin and with their departure, the possible political aspect of the affair was relegated to the back of his mind, especially as he could get no information concerning their interview with the Emperor. The question of restoring the duchy seemed to have entirely dropped out of sight, the general impression prevailing that the Emperor had denied the request and that the discomfited claimants had gone back to Brazil. And the murdered robber had been forgotten!

The whole affair was brought sharply back to Rutile's mind, however, by the contents of a letter he received from Miss Byrd about three months after she had left England.

After the usual preliminaries, the letter proceeded:

"I know you must think I have been neglectful of your request to investigate the Ouro Pretos; but I have not really been so. The information you wanted was not altogether easy to obtain; and in getting it I chanced on some things that roused keen interest in me as a newspaper woman.

"You have, of course, heard of the rebellion that has broken out in the southern provinces of Brazil, but I doubt whether you have any accurate information as to its real strength. The Government naturally minimizes it. But it is really very serious.

"Briefly, it is organized and maintained chiefly by the 1,000,000 German immigrants, who form two-thirds of the population of the three southern provinces. With these are a few excitable Brazilians of the class that is always 'agin the government', partly because they hope to gain something for themselves by success and partly because they are naturally prone to fly off the handle.

"The revolution has two prominent leaders; the Count of Ouro Preto, and his son. In Berlin we somehow got an idea that the old man was dead, but he isn't. He is very much alive! It is his wife, the daughter of the duke of Hochstein, through whom your friends claim the duchy, who is dead.

"The old count is all sorts of a man. Like Castro of Venezuela he was a cattle-thief in early days—or so his enemies say—and graduated, through a period of banditism, to political prominence and enormous wealth. He has organized the rebellion and has it working like clockwork.

"You want to know, of course, whether this rebellion has any connection with Germany and with the request of Ouro Preto to the Kaiser. I think it has! So far as I can find out, there was no rumor of rebellion among the Germans here till young Ouro Preto got back two months ago; there was some discontent, of course, but not enough to account for an outbreak. This fact, however, by itself amounts to little. Nor is the prominence of the Ouro Pretos in the movement particularly significant, although of course, it is cumulative. What is more important, however, is that half a dozen German officers, whose names I will add at the end of this letter, are here training and leading the rebels. You might find out whether they are still carried on the rolls of the German army, and if not, why not?

"Another significant fact is that the rebels are being supplied with munitions of war from Germany. At least three steamers recently arrived from Hamburg loaded with all sorts of war materials. I know this to be a fact. You know how strict the Germans are when they want to be and how impossible it would be for three vessels to get away from German ports on filibustering expeditions without the connivance of the authorities. It would be interesting if you should be able to trace those arms and should find out that they came from government stores, wouldn't it?

"Taken separately, you see these things prove nothing; taken together, they indicate that something is up. Just what it is, I don't know. Do you?

"Being on the inside, so to speak, you may know why the Kaiser might want to cause trouble in Brazil. I confess I can't see his object. And I can't see what difference it makes to the United States—except as a basis for a newspaper story, which, by the way, I have not written. There's self sacrifice for you.

"(N. B. If things get a little more exciting, I'll have to use it, so watch out.)

"By the way, the countess seems not to be in Brazil and I can't find out where she is. She didn't come back with her brother."

After Rutile read this letter, he made inquiries as to the German officers whose names Miss Byrd had added, and found that they had all resigned from the German army about three months before—two days after Ouro Preto's interview with the Kaiser. Returning to his office after ascertaining this fact, he sought the ambassador and laid the facts before him.

His Excellency was a tall, polished, elderly gentleman, who dressed immaculately and walked very straight. He had been a professor of dead languages in a fresh-water college in early youth, had inherited a fortune, and had used it so shrewdly that a grateful president had selected him as minister to a small European power. After three years in that post, a new president had come into office and was about to dispense with his services, when he calmly requested to be transferred to Berlin as ambassador. Before the President had gotten over his amazement the would-be ambassador brought such influence to bear that the President hastened to make the appointment requested—lest a worse thing befall. Since then His Excellency had let Rutile run the business of the office while he himself had bettered the American record by spending more than ten times his salary and allowance in keeping up the dignity of his office. Rutile knew all this and knew that his Excellency would be the last man in the world to be rude enough to pry unnecessarily into the secrets of the government to which he was commissioned.

But he also felt reasonably sure that if he could convince the ambassador that there was real need of action, His Excellency would revert to the shirt-sleeve methods of the early American representatives, let the consequences to his social standing be what they might. But he would be hard to convince.

Rapidly Rutile recited the facts as he knew them. When he had finished, he paused for an instant.

"Well?" demanded His Excellency, placing his finger tips together and leaning back in the professorial attitude he had never lost. "Well, Mr. Rutile! You have stated your premises clearly. Now draw your deductions."

Rutile reached out his hand and spun on its axis the great globe that stood by the desk. "Here is the danger spot," he said, placing his finger on a particular spot.

The ambassador leaned forward. "Brazil?" he inquired.

"Southern Brazil," corrected the secretary. "To speak exactly, the state of Rio Grande do Sul. The total population of that state is 2,000,000 of whom half are Germans or the children of Germans. Your Excellency understands that Brazil is Wilhelm's last chance for a great German colony. All the rest of the valuable world had been collected and labelled by one or the other of the other great powers before Germany felt the need of expansion. Think a minute. What has Germany got? She's got a slice or two of Africa, populated chiefly by niggers, mosquitoes, and soldiers. There aren't any colonists there! She's got a few miscellaneous islands about as big as a Kansas kitchen garden and good for nothing but naval stations. She's got a few square miles of China, good enough for trade but no good at all for settlement. And year after year she sees millions of the best people the Lord made—I'm part

German myself and I know—pouring into the United States and into Brazil just because they haven't got any German colony to go to. Don't you know it gravels the Kaiser? Wouldn't it gravel us? Wouldn't we conspire and work and bluff and fight if need be to get the last piece of territory going before it was too late—But your Excellency knows all this as well as I do."

The ambassador nodded. "Of course I know Germany needs real colonies," he agreed. "Everybody knows that. Witness how near she came to fighting France over Morocco. Of course she'd like to have Brazil, or part of it. But she can't have it. The Monroe Doctrine keeps her out unless she is willing to fight, and it's too absurd to suppose that the Kaiser would deliberately go to war with the United States. Do you really think he would?" The ambassador's tones were incredulous.

Rutile shook his head slowly. "I'm not so sure," he declared. "What is she building all these dreadnoughts for?"

"England! Of course! At least England thinks so."

"Of course she does! Is there anything in the world that Britain does not take to herself? She thinks Wilhelm is aiming at her and he lets her think so. He doesn't mind. But why on earth should he be aiming at her? What has he to gain?"

His Excellency smiled. He was enjoying himself mightily. Nothing in his experience with Rutile had led him to suspect that personage of this sort of thing. He had always looked upon the secretary merely as a perfectly trained automaton who always knew the right thing to do and did it without fuss, and he had been content to leave official business altogether in his capable hands, and to confine himself to the promotion of that cordiality between the two nations that follows a well-cooked dinner. And here was this perfectly trained automaton lecturing him like a schoolboy.

"Doesn't she want territory?" he asked.

"Territory!" Rutile was growing excited. "Just think what Your Excellency is suggesting!" he cried. "Germany today has a fleet less than half as powerful as that of England, and it will be many a long day before she can match her. England is wailing today, not because Germany is overtaking her on the sea, but because she fears she may not be able to remain as powerful as Germany and the second strongest sea power combined. So the result of any war that Germany may wage against England will be more than doubtful. And if she wins she will gain only worthless territory or territory settled by English. On the other hand suppose she is aiming at Brazil. In a few months she will be as strong on the sea as the United States, which alone stands between her and Brazil. Does your Excellency see no significance in a German rebellion in South Brazil aided by German officers and German filibusters?"

The ambassador smiled. "Not much, I'm afraid," he replied, indulgently. "You are more excitable than I supposed, my dear fellow. The Emperor wants Brazil, of course; there's nothing new in that. I've read a dozen newspaper stories about it. But none of them ever came true. And none ever will."

"But—"

The ambassador rose. "What do you want me to do, Rutile?" he asked, seriously.

The secretary hesitated. "I wanted you to send a scarce-story to Washington," he answered at last. "But I see you wouldn't care to stand for it. So I should like permission to run down to Hamburg and see what I can learn about those shipments of arms. Mr. Cox can easily attend to my duties while I am gone. May I have your permission, sir?"

"Certainly! Certainly! Act on your best judgement. And if you can bring me any definite proof, my boy, I'll act on it. You can rely on me."

CHAPTER XVII

With a disgusted grunt, McNew, editor and proprietor of the New York Gazette, flung himself back in his chair. He was impatient by nature, and since he had bought the Gazette and made it the most notorious if not the most famous paper in New York, he had stopped concealing the fact. It is a bad thing for some men to succeed too soon in life. If McNew could have put off his success for twenty years, it would probably not have done him half the harm it did when he was thirty-five.

McNew had succeeded, so he had no patience with failure, not even with the temporary failure that comes to all newspaper men at times. His idea was that all information naturally belonged to the Gazette. Sometimes it was wilfully kept from it by perverse persons, and anon it was maliciously stolen from it by rivals; in either case he held that the loss was due to the failure of the Gazette men. McNew never admitted the impossibility of getting a piece of news.

In the present case he took no pains to hide his disgust.

"So far as I can make out, Risdon," he jeered. "Your trouble seems to lie in the depraved desire of certain people to keep their business to themselves instead of telling it to you. What I want to know is, why do you let them do it? What in hell's bells do you think the Gazette brought you back from Germany and landed you in Washington for? What do you think it pays you for? To report pink teas?"

Risdon flushed, but not from embarrassment. Risdon had been a newspaper writer too long to be readily embarrassed, even by his employer. But he was very angry. He leaned forward and brought his fist down with a bang on the table. "See here, Mac," he began, furiously. "If—"

McNew drew in his horns a little. He wanted to stir up Risdon, but he did not want to stir him too far. "Aw! don't call me Mac," he interrupted. "It's too infernally formal. Call me Johnny."

A reluctant smile curved the corners of Risdon's mouth. He and McNew had known each other ever since they had been cub reporters on the Alta California twenty years ago, and they understood each other thoroughly. "All right, Johnny," he answered, still a little huffily. "If you want my resignation, you can get it."

"What would I do with it?" retorted the other. "I can get a better scoop without turning around. I don't want resignations; I want news. I'm publishing a newspaper, and I want something to fill it. Particularly, I want to know what the German and Japanese ambassadors are discussing so often and so earnestly with the daughter of the governor of the most Germanic state of all the states of Brazil. I don't want pipe dreams; I want facts, f-a-c-t-s, facts, and not a lot of rot like this;" McNew crumpled a dozen typewritten pages in his hand, and flung them contemptuously on the table. "You call yourself a newspaper man and can't find out a little thing like that?" he finished scornfully.

"Little thing! Humph! It is all right to talk, and it's easy enough to invent plots a la Oppenheim, but—"

"Why don't you invent 'em, then," retorted the editor; "instead of sending in rehash like this. How many times have the Japs seized the Philippines—in the newspapers? How many times has Germany made faces at us since Admiral Diedrich tried to bluff Dewey at Manila eight years ago? Pah! It's gotten to be a joke and a mighty bad joke, too; and it isn't helped out much by the row over the schools in San Francisco. Japan isn't going to war, and if she was going to war she wouldn't give us warning that she was getting her back up. She'd jump right in, and fuss about it later. A yarn like this is altogether too fakey!"

Risdon studied the other for a moment. "You don't see any significance in the Germany and Japan ambassadors meeting with a Brazilian countess, then, don't you?" he asked.

"Mighty little. Where's the connection? What's Germany stand to win? As for Brazil—Well! the founding of a German empire in Brazil—if that's what you've got in mind—is about as mouldy as the Japanese attack on the Philippines. This panatella countess is half a German, and it's entirely natural that she should run with the German crowd here. As for the Japs—Well! that may be only a coincidence. Anyway! there's no proof that would warrant me in risking half a dozen great big libel suits. No! No! Risdon! If you want to run a yarn like this you've got to have some real facts to back it up. Why don't you get them?"

Risdon flung up his hands. "How can I?" he demanded. "I've done my best. You know what these embassies are. No one can break into them except a burglar—"

"Then turn burglar!"

"Not even a burglar, I should have said. No subordinate will talk; and I can fancy what Bildstein or Siuki would say if I went to either of them and asked to be told the subjects of their conferences with the Countess Elsa."

"Well! What would they say?"

"Say? They'd say: 'Such a question, sir, is an unwarranted impertinence. You will kindly excuse me.' Then they would show me to the door and would cut me dead the next time they met me! Thank you! I've got to get news in Washington, and I'm not quarreling with my sources of information— especially when I know it wouldn't do any good."

"Well! How about this countess woman? You ought to be used to the aristocracy by now. Can't you break in there, or shall I go back to New York and send an office boy down to show you how?"

Risdon bristled up. "See here, Mac," he exclaimed. "You've said about enough. I'm tired of it, and if you keep on I'm likely to chuck you and my job into the street together. I've tried to do exactly what you suggest. The countess had been here some time before I knew it. When I heard of her, I suspected something was up; I had met the lady in Berlin and had reason to believe she was framing up something. She's staying at Senator Pratt's, and the darkey who runs my errands is sweet on one of the maids there. He told me of her interviews with the German ambassador. Then I saw Pratt and everybody else—Great Scott! Don't you suppose I know my business! Nothing doing! I couldn't get a line. So I went to see the countess. Nothing doing again. I knew there wouldn't be. That woman can give me cards and spades and beat me. She's wasted in Washington and in this age. She ought to have lived in France a hundred years ago. She's a woman to overturn a government—or create one. And I am not so sure she isn't doing one or both. But I can't prove it."

"How does she come to be visiting Pratt?"

"Put-up job! That's one thing that makes me think there's something big brewing. Pratt and his daughter were in Europe last summer just after—well, just after something peculiar happened—and the countess laid herself out for them. The Ouro Pretos aren't any cheap adventurers, you understand. They're all to the mustard in Paris and Berlin, and they made things mighty delightful for Susy Pratt. Now Susy's all right. She's a mighty sweet girl and the senator is—well—he's chairman of the big foreign affairs committee of the Senate, but otherwise he's what you'd expect a senator from his state to be. Fine people, both of them, but not the sort that the countess would lay herself out for without a lot better reason than their sterling characters. The colored gentleman in the wood-pile didn't appear till this winter when the countess cabled from Tokio—Tokio, mind you—asking for an invitation to Washington for the winter. Of course, she got it, and I'd give something to know what she wanted it for. If it's some big political scheme, as I think it is, the chairman of the foreign affairs committee is a mighty good stalking horse to do business behind. I believe she deliberately picked Pratt as a standing guarantee of her innocence and as an unsuspicious somebody whom she could wrap around her finger. Maybe she's right about Pratt's subserviency, but I'm none too sure of it."

McNew considered. Then he slowly gathered up the typed pages that he had thrown on the table. "Then you really believe there's something in this yarn of yours?" he asked.

Risdon did not answer at once. Instead, he stared out of the window along the broad stretch of Pennsylvania Avenue to where half a dozen electric lights branched beneath a pillared portico. So long he stared that McNew's impatience burst out.

"Well! Well! Well!" he shouted. "Why don't you speak?"

Risdon roused himself. "Yes," he said, slowly. "I think it is correct—if not accurate. Of course, it isn't new. It's been used before. In fact, we've been yelling wolf a whole lot and nobody has ever taken it seriously, but the wolf did come at last in the fable, you'll remember, and so may the Japs. I didn't send that yarn just to make a story. I sent it because I really believed that the wolf might be about ready to come and I hoped to scare him off."

McNew laughed. "Lord! you're innocent," he jeered. "Do you really think a scare-head in the Gazette would make the Japs—or Germans either—change their plans—if they have any. Your story would simply warn them. If you're right—if you're the least little bit right, you've got your finger on *the* story of the year. And you go off half cocked. Heavens! Risdon! If I didn't know to the contrary I'd think you a rank cub."

"Tha-a-anks! But suppose war comes—while I wait. Do you want that?"

"War!" McNew shuddered. "God forbid! The Spanish War wiped out the Gazette's entire profits for 1898, and a war with Germany would ruin it."

Risdon nodded. "So I understand," he answered. "I wrote that article, if you'll notice, so as to convey the idea that I got my information from the State Department and that it was prepared for anything. In other words I tried to make it appear that the United States had chosen me to serve formal notice on the Japs to go slow. But I didn't get my information from the State Department. I got the basis of it in Berlin last summer, and I've got more later from various sources. There is really something big on. I was sure of it months ago. That's why I persuaded you to send Miss Byrd to South America. It wasn't for commercial reasons, as I let on—though she's made good on those all right. It was because I was sure there was something doing. But—well, I've gotten frightened. You've read this story"—he pointed to the typed sheets—"and you know what it says. That rebellion in South Brazil is growing stronger day by day. The rebels are getting men and money and arms from unknown sources. Rutile—he's secretary of our embassy in Berlin—

thought they were sent from Germany and got a leave of absence and set off to investigate them. He's disappeared and I can't learn what's become of him. It looks to me as if the game was getting near a finish. I don't know what the State Department knows or thinks; and I've been afraid to ask questions for fear I'd give the scoop away. So it seemed best to print the yarn. If it does nothing else, it may at least stir up the State Department. A yarn like that is more effective when it's published—even if it's published in a yellow sheet like the Gazette. Somehow people put more credence in it. Besides, I think it's not a bad story."

McNew snorted. "Oh! it's good enough, in one way," he admitted. "I've been joshing you to a certain extent. If I had been sure the story was a plain fake, I would have printed it this morning. But I wasn't sure! I have information from—well, from abroad—that makes me think that maybe you're right. That's why I held it up last night. That's why I came down here today. And that's why you're going to come with me and meet the young woman who I hope will help to solve the problem." He drew out his watch and glanced at it. "It's eight o'clock," he noted; "and I wired her that we would call at eight thirty. So get your hat and come along."

CHAPTER XVIII

For the twentieth time Miss Eleanor Byrd peered out of the second story front window, and turned back with a sigh to where her aunt sat in the soft glow of the lamp.

"What can he want, auntie? What can he want?" she repeated, also for the twentieth time.

The elder Miss Byrd did not speak for an instant. "I hope he doesn't want *anything*," she burst out at last. "I wish you had never written to him. It is bad enough that your sister should be connected with that awful paper of his—"

"Now, auntie!" Nellie's eyes danced. "Now, auntie, did you ever see a copy of the Gazette in your life? Honestly, now?"

Miss Byrd flushed—a lovely pink flush, like that of a Dresden shepherdness grown old. "Of course not," she answered indignantly. "Of course not. Your grandfather would never allow me to read papers of that sort—"

"Of what sort, auntie," innocently.

"Of *that* sort," returned Miss Byrd decisively. "It's terrible that Lillian should write for it. No one who conducts a paper like that can be a gentleman! Look what the President has said about him! He has branded him as undesirable— undesirable—and my own niece writes to such a man. And he ventures to telegraph—telegraph—to make an appointment with her."

Nellie laughed softly. She began to say something; then jumped up and ran to the window and peered out behind the edge of the blind. An instant later she came back.

"Another false alarm, auntie!" she said. "Maybe you're going to have your wish, and he won't come at all. But"—she paused and suddenly dropped on her knees beside the elder woman's chair. "Dear auntie," she murmured, softly. "I'm sorry! I'm so sorry to grieve you. I know you don't approve of what Lillian is doing—"

"Nellie!" Miss Lee's tone was shocked.

"Oh! It's true, auntie. You're always thinking that gentlewomen don't do such things and yet you are always perfectly certain that Lilly must be a gentlewoman because she is a Byrd. Well! auntie! Neither Lilly nor I are gentlewomen. We may be ladies—I hope we are—but we're not gentlewomen. There are no gentlewomen in these days. They went out of existence with crinoline—except where they survive in such delightful creatures as you. No gentlewoman earns her own living, and Lilly and I have got to earn ours. Times have changed, auntie, dear! This branch of the Byrd family is poor, dead poor. Lilly threw herself into the breach and is making lots of money, while I barely starve along. I'm tired of it, and if Mr. McNew wants my services, he can have them, at a price." A twinkle came into the girl's eyes. "I hope he won't want me to go a-burgling, and then tell what it feels like," she finished.

"Nellie!"

"Oh! I was only joking, you dear old thing!"

"I know, dear!" returned the older lady, plaintively. "But do you think it's quite proper to jest on such subjects? I can't bear to think of such a thing. Oh! if you—" She broke off as the front bell rang, loudly and insistently.

Nellie Byrd sprang to her feet.

"It's they," she cried, darting to the door. Then she came back. "Dear auntie!" she breathed. "It's all right. Don't worry." Then she tripped down the stairs to admit her visitors.

McNew entered first—a big rough-looking man with a pointed beard. "Miss Byrd?" he questioned.

"Yes! You are Mr. McNew, I suppose. Won't you come in?"

Mr. McNew strode in. "This is Mr. Risdon, Miss Byrd," he explained. "He tries to run the Gazette's Washington office."

Miss Byrd's eyes rested kindly on the correspondent. "I know Mr. Risdon by sight," she explained. "No one could be a social secretary in Washington without knowing him. My sister Lillian has written me about him, too. Won't you sit down, gentlemen?"

"Thank you!" Risdon drew forward a chair and the three disposed themselves.

McNew wasted no time in preliminaries. He was a busy man, and had no time to spare.

"Miss Byrd," he began, as soon as he was seated. "Some time ago I received an application from you for work? Do you still want it?"

Miss Byrd nodded. "Very much," she said. "I hope you have some for me."

"That depends! Your sister has done very good work for the Gazette. Risdon here suggested sending her to South America. He and she both fooled me; they got me to send her for one thing, and they arranged for her to do another. But she's done both very well."

"I'm glad!"

"That's one reason why I'm inclined to give you a chance. I am told that you speak German fluently, Miss Byrd."

Nellie nodded. "About as well as I do English," she declared.

"Very good! If you will apply tomorrow to Senator Pratt—you know his address—he will engage you as his daughter's social secretary at twenty-five dollars a week. The Gazette will pay you forty dollars more."

Nellie Byrd's pale face bloomed with sudden vivid color. McNew staring at her, read her thoughts, and smiled grimly. He enjoyed startling people.

"What's the matter?" he demanded.

Nellie's color receded, leaving her pale. She looked at McNew thoughtfully, apparently trying to fathom him.

"I hoped you could give me a chance to try something besides acting as social secretary," she syllabled, slowly. "But beggars mustn't be choosers. I understand the twenty-five dollars, but why the forty. What service do I render the Gazette when I am acting as social secretary for Senator Pratt."

McNew watched the light coming and going behind the girl's clear blue eyes. "For the forty dollars," he answered, slowly. "I wish you to watch and report to me every act of the Countess del Ouro Preto, who is spending the winter with Miss Pratt? Will you do it?"

"No!" If Nellie Byrd was disappointed, she concealed the fact well. Her voice came as calm as ever. "You are mistaken in me, Mr. McNew. I am not a spy."

"Why not?" McNew shot the question at her. "Why not? Why not? Tell me why not."

"It is not honorable."

"Honorable! Honorable! Was Nathan Hale dishonorable? Was Major Andree dishonorable?"

Miss Byrd shook her head. "They were soldiers. What they did they did for their country. That fact glorified their acts. They were not newspaper spies."

McNew hitched his chair forward. His eyes glowed. "Miss Byrd," he said, slowly. "In watching the Countess del Ouro Preto you will probably be doing a service to your country scarcely less than that of a spy in a war. You will not be risking death, but you will be risking your social standing, which you would probably lose if it became known that you were a Gazette spy. I have reason to believe that the countess is the channel of communication between the German and the Japanese Ambassadors in a plot to humiliate the United States—perhaps to involve it in war. I want to know the truth; I want to know it in order to get an exclusive story for the Gazette. But I want still more to know it for the sake of the United States. The Monroe doctrine—But Risdon will explain that to you."

Miss Byrd turned to Risdon while McNew leaned back and watched the changes flit over her delicate face as the younger man talked. A new shade of earnestness, altogether charming, crept over it toward the end.

Risdon went over the situation as he understood it to exist. He told of the petition of the Ouro Pretos to the Emperor and its supposed result; of the rebellion that broke out shortly afterwards in Brazil; of the visit (reported by a Gazette correspondent) of the Countess to Japan; of her return to the United States and of her alleged conferences with the Japanese and German ambassadors; and called attention to the growing excitement in California growing out of the strike and boycott that was being enforced against the Japanese restaurants, and out of the denial of public school privileges to the Japanese in San Francisco.

McNew broke in. "Your sister," he said, "has sent some incendiary yarns from Brazil—which I have not printed. Yesterday she cabled the worst of all. She's on her way home now, by the way."

Nellie's eyes brightened. "Oh! is she?" she cried. "I'm so glad. I didn't know."

"Nobody knew. Risdon here didn't know till he heard me tell you. And it's just as well to talk about it. It mightn't do any harm and again it might. She's coming on the same ship with Ouro Preto!"

"Oh!" Miss Byrd's tones were significant and not altogether approving.

But McNew settled back in his chair. "Go on, Risdon," he ordered.

Risdon resumed. "There really isn't much more to say," he declared. "Altogether the circumstances are very suspicious. Singly they amount to nothing, together they may amount to a good deal. The countess is a very clever woman, and we believe that she is the mainspring of the plot and is doing some very important work in connection with it in this country, and we want to find out what this work is."

Miss Byrd had followed the argument closely. "And then?" she questioned, calmly, when Risdon finished.

"Then we will print it. It will be a great scoop for the Gazette, of course. But it may also mean salvation for the country."

"And," broke in McNew, "You don't want to run away with the idea that you are betraying your employer. Old Pratt will know what your errand in his house is."

"Oh!" Miss Byrd's face cleared. "That changes the case," she conceded.

"Of course! You see Risdon here got scared, and wired a lot of stuff last night that brought me down to Washington in a hurry. I saw Pratt this morning and reasoned with him. He's willing enough to oblige the Gazette, Pratt is. Besides, he had his suspicions already. Pratt's no fool, you understand. No fool ever gets to be United States Senator nowadays. Pratt's got the far west idea of women, and he doesn't understand the type of the countess. She doesn't understand him either, however. So it's a stand off. The upshot is that he agreed to my terms. He won't discuss it with you, though! To him you will be his daughter's social secretary and nothing else, and you've got to attend to your duties as such; what else you may do he doesn't care. Now— Will you do it?"

McNew rose, and Miss Byrd did so also. "Yes," she said, slowly. "I will do it!"

"Good! Then the first thing you have to do is to forget that you know German."

CHAPTER XIX

As Miss Eleanor Byrd soon found, her duties as social secretary to Miss Pratt were no sinecure. The Pratts had been in Washington thirteen years, the Senator having just started on his third term in the upper house of the national government, but they had not cared much for social affairs until their daughter was ready to make her bow to society. Then they discovered, to their amazement, that while they could command a certain amount of consideration as a senator's family, there were yet many circles into which they could not penetrate. These circles, although really little if any better than those to which they had access, naturally became at once exceedingly desirable to both Mrs. Pratt and her daughter. Especially did they desire, as all Washington women do, to get into the diplomatic set, and when chance—they thought it was chance—threw the Countess Elsa in their way, they were ready to grapple her to themselves with hooks of steel—or gold. When, instead of making demands upon them, the countess appeared to lay herself out to please them, they were overjoyed; and when she proposed to visit them in their Washington home, their delight knew no bounds; even Senator Pratt, hard-headed business man as he was, was pleased, but partly because the countess always treated him with a consideration as grateful as it is rare to the average American father and husband. It was Senator Pratt who a few months before had openly thanked God that he didn't keep a dog. "Because," he said, "my wife comes first, my daughter second, and if we kept a dog, I'd come fourth."

Pleased the Senator was, but not carried beyond his depths. Life-long habits are strong, and more than once he had asked himself what there was "in it" for the countess. When McNew offered an answer, his suggestion fell on fertile ground.

But he wanted a quid pro quo, nevertheless. If he paid Miss Byrd $100 a month to manage his daughter's social affairs, he wanted her to earn the money. And as neither his daughter nor his wife had any idea as to the social secretary's real mission, she found her hands full.

A week passed without significant event—or at least without event that seemed significant to Miss Byrd. Twice a week the ladies served tea informally to all who liked to drop in, and on these occasions the members of the various legations and embassies were always present in good numbers. But they clustered around Miss Pratt—who was both pretty and interesting—almost as numerously as they did about the countess, although the latter had been the attraction that had drawn them to the house. The talk was necessarily polyglot, though mostly in either French or English, but so far as Miss Byrd could see, the countess indulged in no private conversations with any one. What she did when away from home Miss Byrd could not always tell, for of course she was not invited to many of the entertainments attended by the countess and Miss Pratt. However, she knew that McNew had other spies there.

As the days went by, the anxiety of those who were watching grew apace. The rebels in Brazil were steadily becoming more and more powerful, and the German newspapers were advocating their recognition as belligerents.

The Japanese were growing more insistent in their demands. Some of the papers were clamoring for war. If there was really anything in the supposed plot, the crisis must be drawing near.

Thinking over it all, Risdon made up his mind that the arrival of Ouro Preto, who was still speeding northward, would be followed by important events. And still no clue could be discovered.

At last, however, partial enlightenment came. The Pratt parlors had been crowded that afternoon, but the crowd had thinned out until only half a dozen callers remained. Three of these were grouped around Miss Pratt, and the other three around the countess. With a sudden shock Miss Byrd, sitting at the tea table noticed that these latter three were the German and Japanese ambassadors and the latter's wife; suddenly she remembered that the last, though for forty years married to a Japanese, was German by birth.

As she bent her face over the teacups, to hide the flush that rose in her cheeks at the sudden realization of what this might mean, the countess leaned toward the Japanese ambassador. "Did you see Maude Adams last night, Baron?" she asked. "How do you like her?" Then without the slightest change in her sprightly tones she slipped into German; "and, Baron," she questioned; "when do you present your demands to the President?"

In spite of herself, Miss Byrd started. Instantly she realized that here was the unsuspected channel of communication. Relying on the ignorance of the rest of the household of rapid vernacular German, the countess, with insolent daring, had done her plotting under the eyes of everybody.

But the Japanese ambassador was speaking, and there was no time for considering other things.

"Charming!" he said in English; but—he changed to German—"I shall never present them."

The countess showed no vexation. "Isn't she?" she asked. "Why not?" in German.

"She assuredly is. I wanted to see her in Joan of Arc, but my duties kept me here. Because," in German, "I have convinced my government that this country is its best friend and have conveyed to it the assurance of the President that he will see that my countrymen in California receive all their treaty rights." "You did not go either, Countess, did you?" in English.

"No! I was too busy. And your excellency!" She turned to the German ambassador. "What do you think of her?"

The German scowled. "I do not like her," he sputtered; "but she has many friends. I suppose your ideas are fixed, Baron, and that no argument could possibly alter them."

The Jap shook his head. "None!" he answered. "My opinion is absolutely fixed!"

"Then—But I am making an unconscionably long stay. I leave the Baron in your hands, countess. Perhaps you may persuade him."

The countess smiled mysteriously. "Perhaps," she said. "Perhaps!"

That night Miss Byrd left the house and hurried down to Risdon's office; and laid the story before him. When she got back she learned that the countess was suffering with a headache and had decided not to go out that night. The next day her maid reported that she was still feeling badly. That afternoon a doctor—the doctor attached to the German embassy—was called in. The countess, however, did not improve. She kept her room and begged to be excused from seeing any one—even Miss Pratt. It was not until five days later that Miss Byrd suspected that she was no longer in the house. But by that time the countess was three thousand miles away from Washington.

CHAPTER XX

Walter Topham was nearing San Francisco. His stay in Japan had been very brief. Long before he had had time to become acquainted with conditions in that country or to make certain that Stiles' suspicions as to intense activity in the Japanese arsenals and dockyards were justified, the ambassador had called him into his private office and thrust before him a dispatch from Washington from the Secretary of State.

"Ask Topham what he knows about the Countess del Ouro Preto in Berlin. Cable fully," it read.

The query was so unexpected that Topham flushed, despite his effort not to do so and despite his consciousness that the keen eyes of the ambassador were upon him. He flushed, but he did not hasten to answer as most people would have done in his place; instead he read the dispatch again slowly; and concluded that he owed it to what he had told Rutile in Berlin, and to that gentleman's faculty of smelling out intrigues.

"Well, Mr. Topham?" questioned the ambassador.

Topham looked up. "I know the lady," he said, slowly. "I met her in Berlin, and learned something of her mission there. I met her the night I reached Tokio—perhaps Stiles has told you. I do not want to conceal anything concerning her from any one who has a right to ask. The only question is what the Secretary wants to know."

"Everything! I suppose, Mr. Topham."

"'Everything' is pretty broad. Perhaps I had better write down anything that I have observed that I think may be of interest to the government, and submit it to you. Then if there is anything lacking, perhaps you may be able to discover what it is."

The ambassador nodded. "Do so, Mr. Topham."

Topham wrote out his account carefully, choosing his words with exactitude. He was anxious to tell everything that the secretary could want to know and yet not to magnify any of it or give any part of it a significance that it really did not possess.

He had about come to the conclusion that Stiles was wrong and that the errand of the countess to Japan had nothing whatever to do with any intrigue against the United States, and he naturally did not wish to say anything that would create such a belief. Nor did he consider himself called on to go into his personal relations with the countess.

He gave the paper to the ambassador, who read it, asked no questions, and presumably cabled its substance to Washington. For the next day Topham received orders to leave for Washington on the next steamer.

Loud was Stiles' disgust. "I might have known it," he cried. "It's just like those fellows! They've got about half the navy in Washington already, and want more of it."

"I think they want me for a special reason," suggested Topham.

"Oh! I suppose so. Devilish queer about that countess, isn't it. I wonder what she really was up to!"

Topham looked the secretary in the eye. "Really! if you don't mind, I would rather not discuss her," he observed gently.

"Oh! no offense! Say, look here, Topham. Your going is lucky in one sense, because you can do something for me—and for the government—on your way. Do you remember that Jap colonel—Hakodate his name was—whom you met here the day after your arrival?"

"Yes! I think so."

"Would you know him again?"

"I might. I'm not certain! Why?"

"Well! I told you we had native spies. One of them brought in word this morning that Colonel Hakodate sailed a week ago for San Francisco as an immigrant and that he carried letters to one Hiroshina, who keeps a Jap restaurant on Market Street near Kearny. Of course the man may be lying and of course you may say that there's nothing in it even if he's telling the truth. But it looks dashed funny to me, and I wish you'd just drop in at that restaurant when you get to San Francisco, and snoop around a bit. See if you can spot Hakodate there, and see what he's up to."

Topham promised.

That had been two months before and San Francisco was now close at hand. The glow that hovers above every great city had grown more and more distinct; the peak of Mt. Tamalpais bisected it and the black bulk of the low southern shore was faintly visible beneath it. Soon the channel and range lights grew into visibility. Then the steamer slid through the heavy rolling waves of the bar into the calm of the outer bay. Fifteen minutes more and it passed through the Golden Gate and the great city lay outstretched before it.

Topham looked at his watch and wondered whether he would get ashore in time to catch the midnight train for the east.

Scarcely had he formulated his wish, when a boat came alongside, and a fresh young voice hailed the deck.

"This is a launch from Fort Alcatraz," it explained. "Is Commander Topham on board? I've been sent to land him. Here's the permit from quarantine."

In five minutes Topham was in the boat, speeding shoreward. "Orders from Washington, Mr. Topham," explained the officer in charge. "Your berth has been engaged on the twelve o'clock train. It's nearly nine now. Meanwhile I'm at your orders. Will you come out to the fort, or go straight to Oakland and the train, or do you want to see the Great White Way in San Francisco first? Command me."

"Thank you! I'll go to San Francisco, please. I have an errand to discharge. Please land me at the foot of Market Street."

"Just as you say, sir." The young man spoke to the coxswain and the boat bore away to the right.

Once landed in the western city, Topham said good-night and started up Market Street, reading the signs on the lamp posts as he went.

Stiles had not been able to give him the number of the restaurant for which he was looking, but he knew that it was on Market Street just below Kearney Street, close to Lotta's fountain and the Chronicle Building, which he could see outlined against the sky far up the street.

As he stepped briskly along it occurred to him that there was an unusual stir in the city, though not being familiar with its ordinary state he had no means of comparison. Still, it seemed to him that conditions could not be altogether normal. The people were not moving about their business, but were congregating in groups here and there. Now and then there would be a sudden movement to one point or another, but never for any reason that Topham could see.

As a matter of fact he paid little attention. He was interested in the task that Stiles had set him—a task for which the three hours available before his train left for the east might easily prove anything but superabundant. When at last he caught sight of a brilliant sign "Hiroshima, Japanese restaurant," his faint curiosity as to the crowd disappeared.

But before he could enter the portals of the restaurant a big workingman— nearly as big a man as himself—barred his way.

"You ain't goin' in that Jap hash house, are you, friend?" inquired the stranger.

Topham halted. "That was—er—my idea," he responded. "Why not?"

"There is strike on; see? An' the Japs are boycotted; see? They're playin' the devil with hard-workin' Americans. And we ain't goin' to stand for it. You want to keep away from there, mister."

Topham hesitated. His interlocutor was not alone; half a dozen other men, loafing near, were evidently fellow pickets. Topham did not want any trouble during the few hours he was to be in the city. Yet he was resolved to enter the restaurant. The sight of two policemen on guard at the door decided him to force the game.

"I'm sorry," he said. "But I must go in. There are reasons why I can't forego having my supper there. Pardon me!" He pushed by and stepped to the door. As he went he heard the man cursing behind him.

He seated himself and ordered a meal from a bill of fare presented him by a stocky Japanese waiter, who seemed not at all alarmed by the situation. Perhaps he had grown hardened to it.

When the waiter had disappeared toward the back of the place Topham stared around him.

Whether because of the hour or because of the strike, the restaurant was almost empty. Only two guests beside himself were in the place and neither of these seemed to be enjoying his meal. Another waiter was hovering over them, and behind the cashier's desk sat a Japanese. As Topham looked this man raised his head and the navy officer recognized him. It was Colonel Hakodate.

The thing took away Topham's breath for an instant. Almost he became a convert to Stiles' prognostications of war. For it was inconceivable that a samurai of the bluest Japanese blood, akin to the emperor himself, and an officer of the imperial army, should turn restaurant keeper except for grave reasons.

Little time, however was given him to think. From the street without came a sudden outcry, a sort of chilling yell that brought all in the place to their feet. Another instant a dozen stones crashed through the plate-glass windows. Then came a rush of feet and a crowd of men leaped into the broad doorway. Topham saw the clubs of the two policemen rise and fall like flails, and saw them forced backward, still fighting.

It was all so sudden, so unexpected, that the head of the crowd was actually in the room before he realized what was happening. Then he sprang forward with a yell to the aid of the police.

But he never reached them. The Japs were quicker than he. Before he had taken two steps, he heard the crash of firearms and saw Colonel Hakodate and his two waiters standing coolly up pouring shot after shot into the mass of the mob.

"Banzai! Banzai!" yelled the colonel. "Stand to it, brothers. Remember! It is the emperor's command."

It was only for a second. Then the policemen went down and the mob rolled in. The Japs disappeared, and Topham snatching up a chair, breathlessly defended himself against a score of brawny men who swarmed upon him.

For half a minute he held them at bay. Then a paralyzing blow on the arm sent his chair crashing from his hands and he saw death staring at him from a score of maddened eyes.

But before the blow could fall, a woman burst through the circle and flung herself upon him. One arm she threw around his neck and threw the other up into the faces of the mob.

"All right! boys! All right," she cried. "Standt back. Dieses ist mein mann!"

Topham saw the fire die out of the eyes that circled him. For a moment their owners hesitated; then—

"Hurrah for Dutch Elsie!" yelled one, and the others took up the cry. "Hurrah for Dutch Elsie."

"Out of here. Quick!" the woman was clamoring in the navy man's ear. "Quick. The police are coming. Quick!"

But Topham stood still. "You," he cried. "You!"

"Yes, I! I'll explain later. But come now! Quick! come! Dios! Come!"

And Topham went.

CHAPTER XXI

Life was coming back again into Topham's arm, and by main strength he forced his way through the crowd, making a path to the door for himself and the countess. Once through the aperture, progress was easier, though not too easy, for the crowd outside was packed and jammed about the door. At last, however, he was free, just as the clatter of hoofs on the granite told that the police patrol had arrived.

The countess clung to his arm, but made no attempt to speak. She was dressed plainly, like a factory worker of the poorer class. She looked much older than when he had seen her last, and he guessed that some of the shadows on her face had been purposely put there by skillful hands. Her hair puzzled him at first, but he soon guessed that its grayish tinge was due to powder.

The mob was dispersing, fleeing in all directions, and the police were plowing their way through it toward the wrecked restaurant.

Topham glanced about him, caught sight of the telegraph office that he had noted half an hour before and quickly drew the woman up the steps and inside.

As he turned toward the table with its pile of blanks, she caught him by the arm. "What are you going to do?" she gasped.

Topham looked at her with infinite sadness in his eyes. "I am going to telegraph to the President that the anti-Japanese riots in San Francisco have been provoked by German agents for the purpose of embroiling Japan with the United States for some end that I cannot guess. Afterwards, I should be glad if you can spare me a word. I owe my life to you!"

The countess took no notice at all of his last words. Her attention was concentrated on what had gone before. "You will not send that dispatch!" she pleaded.

"I must. You know that I must."

"But—but—as you say—I saved your life. If it had not been for me you would not be alive to send anything. I think I have the right to ask you not to send it. Please! For my sake!"

The sweat crept out on Topham's forehead, but his tones did not falter. "I must," he answered.

"Yet listen first to me! I have the right to ask you at least to listen." Her voice, deep and rich, had lost none of its intensity, nor her glorious eyes any of their appeal. Topham would have known them anywhere; in fact, it was by them that he had first recognized her when she flung herself upon him. "Grant me at least ten minutes," she begged. "You will not refuse the first thing I ever asked of you!"

Topham glanced up to where a clock face marked the hour. "No!" he said, gently. "I will not refuse to listen to you. But I can give you but little more than the ten minutes you ask. My train leaves in an hour and the ferry is some distance away. I will listen, but I cannot yield. I have been ordered to Washington to tell the President what I know of the Countess de Ouro Preto."

With round eyes the woman stared at him. "So!" she syllabled, under her breath. "So he suspects. *What* does he suspect?" she demanded fiercely.

"I do not know."

"But you can guess."

Topham shook his head. "No," he answered, gently. "I may not guess even if I could. You know that, countess. No one knows it better than you."

Some great emotion seemed to sweep through the woman's frame. She shivered, though the night was not cold; her lips trembled; her eyes stared blankly. Then, quick as it had come, the stress vanished and her features shaped themselves into a mocking smile.

"So," she said, bitingly. "So all those pretty things you said to me in Berlin and in Tokio were false. You amused yourself, perhaps?"

Topham shook his head. "They were true," he affirmed. "They are still true. You know it."

His directness was disconcerting. An appeal to one against one's self usually is. But the scorn in the woman's eyes did not lessen.

"Yet you refuse?"

"Yes! I refuse." A flash of passion trembled in Topham's tones. "God!" he cried. "If I did not have to refuse! If I did not have to refuse!"

Coolly the countess studied him. His agitation was welcome. If it should increase anything was possible. But one cannot argue with a marble statue. For herself the time of self-betrayal was past. Brain had usurped the rule of heart, and would maintain itself till the end.

"So you say," she jeered.

Topham glanced round. The long room was nearly empty, and what occupants it had were collected at the broad windows staring out into the street.

"Countess!" he said, swiftly. "I do not know in what plot you are engaged. I can not conceive what it may be. But I am very certain that any plot in which Germany and Japan are concerned; any plot that leads German emissaries to stir up mobs to murder Japanese in San Francisco—"

"It was not murder," pantingly.

"Was it not? I hope not? But that was the plain intent—"

"No! No! The Japanese knew. They were ordered—" she broke off.

"Of course! I knew that. Colonel Hakodate would not have been there except under orders. Yet it was murder—"

"No! It was war!"

Topham paused. "Perhaps!" he acquiesced, after an instant. "Perhaps! Murder seems to me no less murder when done by the orders of an Emperor. But it is not for me to judge. Nor will I try to question you—not even about the murder at the door of the Embassy in Berlin. God knows I shall have enough to tell the President without taking advantage of your confessions. But anything that can bring about such occurrences as I have seen tonight is a thing that no officer can keep from his chief."

"But—but if I tell you that your President would not be interested? If I tell you that this is not at all an affair for the United States? What then? Will you believe me?"

"Believe you? As a man, yes! As an officer of the United States, no. It is not for me to believe or disbelieve. It is for me to obey. My orders were to cable what I knew. That means that I am to telegraph any later information. But, pardon me, the ten minutes are up. I must write my dispatch and go!"

He turned away, resolutely enough to all appearances. His tones were even and his manner calm. But the countess guessed that beneath the mask his heart was storming madly. She knew men, did the countess Elsa! She had met Topham's quiet sort before.

With a sudden movement she flung her hand across the telegraph blank.

"In Berlin you asked me to marry you," she breathed. "Do you still wish me to do so?"

Topham's eyes flamed. "Marry me! Marry me!" he groaned. "God knows I want it more than—more than—"

"Then do not send that message, and I will marry you at once—within the hour. I will abandon my plans; give up my life work; break my oath to the dead. I will be yours to do with as you will. Only—only I ask—Forget what has happened here tonight. Do not wire it! Do not speak of it! Let it be as if it had never been. Am I not worth it, beloved? Ah! Don't you know that I will make up to you for it all?"

Her face was very near his; her glowing eyes beamed into his; the soft fragrance of her breath fanned his cheeks. But he set his face like flint.

"No!" he said.

"Then tell the President what you like when you see him. But do not telegraph."

"No!"

The countess drew back. "Then," she said, with a break in her voice. "Then— Good-by."

"Good-by?"

"Good-by—forever. That dispatch will mark the end for you and me. I beg! I implore you not to send it. But I warn you, too!"

Slowly but decidedly Topham shook his head. "God help me!" he breathed. "But send it I must!"

Swiftly, as if desiring to put himself beyond the reach of temptation, he snatched up the pen and scribbled a score of hasty words. Then he hurried to the clerk's grating, thrust it in, and turning, staggered blindly toward the door.

But the countess was waiting for him, and in her eyes he saw a light he had never thought to see again. Heedless of who might see she stretched her arms wide.

"Thank God! Oh! Thank God! that there is one true man left," she cried. "I thought all men were liars till you showed me to the contrary. I *had* to try you, beloved! I had to do my best to stop you, and I did do my best. But I was praying all the while that I might fail. And I thank God I did fail. Take me, beloved, and do with me what you will. I can trust you with anything in the world."

CHAPTER XXII

Leeds of the Star was the first of a group to spy McNew as he swung past the pillared portico and turned down the asphalt walk to the office building. Leeds rubbed his eyes and looked again. McNew had not been to the White House for five years—not since the President had declared him morally guilty of murder by his having stirred up the class hatred that had led to it. That he should come there at that late day meant something out of the ordinary.

Leeds was a local man, however, and did not take a very intense interest in the doings of New York newspaper proprietors, no matter how yellow they might be. So he turned to Iverson of the Gazette.

"Isn't that your boss toting an olive branch up the walk?" he inquired.

Iverson jumped up, and glanced where Leeds pointed. Then, with an elaborate assumption of indifference, he strolled to the foot of the steps to meet his chief. His face showed little interest, but Iverson's face had long before ceased to be a mirror of his mind. In reality he was mightily amazed at McNew's coming. So nonchalantly did he move that he had gained a dozen steps before any of the other newspaper men realized the situation. When they did, they tried to catch up with him without appearing to do so.

McNew, however, appeared to have no desire to make a mystery of his coming or to give any exclusive information to his own correspondent. He nodded to him indifferently; then glanced at the other men.

"Good-morning! Good-morning! Gentlemen!" he called. "What do you know?"

Clark of the Post answered him. "Don't know a thing, Mr. McNew. What's the news from New York?"

"Read it in the Gazette," retorted McNew. "Is the president on view today?"

O'Laughlin of the World shook his head. "Nothing doing today," he answered. "Cabinet day, you know, Mr. McNew!"

McNew shrugged his shoulders. "Oh! well!" he remarked. "It doesn't matter. His secretary will do. Sorry, boys! But I haven't a bit of news to give you. I'm here on personal business. Good-morning."

He strove to push through the ring of newspaper men, but they closed up and stood so firm that he would have had to use some force to get away. So he laughed and stood still. "Well, boys?" he questioned.

O'Laughlin caught his eye. "Who carried the flag of truce?" he demanded.

The sunlight glinted through the trees into McNew's eyes, masking the expression that crept into them. "There isn't any flag of truce," he answered slowly. "I am on the same terms with the President today that I was five years ago. I have business here today, however, and I came to transact it with the President or his secretary—not with the man who used his high office to slander me. I did not come to ask any favors or offer any friendship; I merely come to do business. I may not even see the President. I hope I make my position clear?"

The men nodded. "Damned clear," muttered O'Laughlin, but so low that McNew did not hear him.

"Then once more, good-morning, gentlemen." The editor passed through the ring into the building. As he vanished O'Laughlin gazed after him shrewdly; then turned to Black of the Journal. "Wonder what the devil he really is here for?" he muttered.

"The devil knows and he won't split on a pal," misquoted Black. "Cheer up! O'Laughlin! You'll see it all in the Gazette in the morning."

But O'Laughlin did not see it in the Gazette, either on the next or on any other day. McNew's errand at the White House was not for publication.

Passing through the reception hall, with the air of one used to his surroundings, the editor nodded to the colored messenger at an inner door. "Good-morning, Arthur!" he greeted. "Is the secretary at liberty?"

Arthur rose and flung open the door as nimbly as the "rheumatiz" permitted. "Yes, suh! I think so, suh!" he answered. "Walk right in, suh! Ain't nobody yere this mornin'."

McNew stepped in. A glance showed him that no strangers were present, and he strode straight up to a man who sat writing at a desk close beneath the big south windows. Grim lines had suddenly started out in his face, and when he spoke all lightness had vanished from his tones. Any one seeing him then could understand how he could have built his paper up from nothing to be a national power.

"Mr. Secretary," he said. "I must see the President instantly."

The secretary laid down his pen and rose slowly to his feet. In his way he was as strong a character as McNew—not a man to be hurried or stampeded. "Impossible, just now, Mr. McNew," he answered briefly. "After the cabinet meeting, perhaps."

"Nothing is impossible. I must see him at once. The matter is one of the very gravest importance. After the cabinet meeting will be too late."

The secretary hesitated. "Can you tell me your business?" he asked.

"I should rather not. You know, Mr. Loren, none better, that I am no friend of the President's. That I came here at all is evidence that my errand is important. That I come at such a time ought to be evidence that it is of national and not merely of personal importance. I want one minute's speech with the President. After that, he can go back to the cabinet meeting—if he wants to. This is serious, Mr. Secretary! Very serious!"

The secretary rose briskly. When he gave way, he gave way absolutely. There was no half-way surrender about Loren. "I'll tell the President," he conceded, as he passed to an inner door; "on your head be the consequences."

In a moment the President bustled in. Curtly he nodded to McNew. "You want to see me, Mr. McNew?" he questioned, brusquely.

"Yes! Read this, please."

Neither man troubled to show much courtesy. Each hated the other with a cordial hatred that caused any meeting between them to resemble that between two bulldogs ready yet hesitating to fly at each other. McNew had published vitriolic things about the President and the President had retorted more calmly but more bitterly. Each really considered the other a menace to the country.

Further, the President was vexed at being interrupted. Theoretically cabinet meetings are affairs of tremendous dignity, not to be lightly intruded upon. Actually, if rumor speaks true, their importance is sometimes in inverse ratio to their secrecy.

Nevertheless, the President took the paper that McNew extended to him, and ran his eye down it. The look of suspicion faded from his face; and he read it again more slowly. Then he looked up.

"The importance of this lies more in what it infers than in what it says," he asserted, sternly; "and both depend on who wrote it. I do not recognize the signature."

McNew nodded. "It is a cipher signature," he explained. "The whole message came in cipher. The writer is Miss Lillian Byrd, formerly of this city. You know her, I believe."

The President nodded. "I know her very well," he said, "and I have the greatest confidence in anything she may say. Where is she? How did she come to send such a message?"

"She is a Gazette correspondent. She has been doing some work in South America for the Gazette. You may have read her dispatches from there. They have been very significant. Three weeks ago she left Buenos Ayres for New York on the steamer Southern Cross. Last night she sent this dispatch by wireless in code via Guantanamo. I got it in New York at three o'clock this morning and left for Washington with it an hour later on a special train."

"You have not published it?"

"No."

"Why not? It is a good story. It would cause a sensation. Why do you not publish it, Mr. McNew?"

McNew's atramentous face grew darker. "Because, Mr. President," he grated; "because I am an American like yourself. I know, Mr. President, that you think I cater to anarchy for the sake of money. I think that you—But, no matter; I did not come here to bandy words. Frankly, I dislike you, Mr. President, and I would never have brought that message to you if any other course had been possible. I distrust your policies and disapprove your acts. But you are President and the subject matter of that dispatch clearly falls within your province. Therefore I bring it to you. Take it, not as the service of a friend but merely as that of one who is willing for the moment to sink personal enmity for the sake of his country."

The President listened quietly while the editor spoke.

"Agreed," he answered. "We will work together in this; later if need be we can again lock horns. You have done neither more nor less than your duty, Mr. McNew. On its face this dispatch," he slapped it across his hand—"this dispatch is incredible. As a theme for an Oppenheim romance it would be admirable. As a yellow-journal feature story it might sell a few copies of the Gazette. It would not do more. The only people who would believe it would be those who already know it to be true—if it is true. Yet—if it is true—to publish it would do great harm, for it would show these very people that we know something of their plans. So I will ask you to suppress it altogether. I will see that you get another scoop to balance this one. I will tell you that I believe it is true. I received other information only last night that convinces me. Now, Mr. McNew, I must see Miss Byrd at the earliest possible moment."

McNew nodded. "I thought so," he answered. "That was why I insisted on seeing you at once. Miss Byrd's steamer ought to pass outside the capes of the Chesapeake bound for New York some time tonight. Can you send a torpedo boat or a cruiser out to intercept her?"

The President turned to his secretary. "Ask Secretary Metson to come here, Mr. Loren," he ordered.

Loren slipped into the cabinet room. In an instant he was back. Close behind him came a stout, sandy-mustached man, who nodded to McNew with an air of surprise.

The President, however, allowed no time for explanations. "Mr. Metson," he questioned, instantly. "Have we any small vessels at Hampton Roads that can go to sea without delay."

Metson nodded. "Four or five, I believe," he answered promptly. "Two destroyers, one gun-boat, one protected cruiser—"

"Order the swiftest to be ready to leave the instant an officer reaches her with orders. Can you put your hand on Commander Topham, whom you brought to me last night, or is he out of reach?"

Metson looked undecided. "I think he is in the navy department now," he asserted. "If Mr. Loren will telephone over—"

"Do so, Loren."

Topham was easily found, and in less than five minutes was in the room.

The President went straight to the point. "Mr. Topham," he said. "An American lady, Miss Byrd, a correspondent of the Gazette, will pass the entrance of Chesapeake Bay on the steamship Southern Cross some time tonight. I want you to take train—a special if need be"— He broke off. "Find out about trains, and order a special at once, if necessary, Mr. Loren," he flung over his shoulder. Then: "You will proceed immediately to Fortress Monroe, Mr. Topham," he resumed; "go on board a torpedo boat that will be waiting, intercept the ship, and bring Miss Byrd here at the earliest possible moment. She will probably be willing to come. If not, you must try to persuade her."

"She will come, Mr. President. I know her personally."

"So much the better. I am sending you, Mr. Topham, because of your connection with the case. The Count of Ouro Preto is on board the Southern Cross. He must not be allowed to interfere."

"He shall not be, sir."

"Miss Byrd sent this dispatch to the Gazette by wireless last night. Mr. Loren will give you a copy of it. From the position of the vessel at that time, you can calculate where she will be tonight. Probably you can locate her by wireless. Do you understand?"

"Fully, sir."

"Then consult with Mr. Loren and Mr. Metson, and go. Lose no time."

CHAPTER XXIII

Leaning alternately to right and to left to meet the roll of the ship, Ouro Preto made his way along the deck of the Southern Cross, his eyes fixed on a vacant chair by Lillian Byrd's side. Miss Byrd saw him coming, and longed to escape, but could not do so.

She did not wish to talk with the count, although she had come on board the Southern Cross at Buenos Ayres for the express purpose of obtaining from him certain knowledge that she felt sure that he possessed. For three weeks she had been working, quietly and unobtrusively but effectively, to gain it, and when she saw him approaching she felt that success was about to crown her efforts.

Yet in that moment of prospective triumph contrition seized her, and she looked down, panic-stricken, striving to gain time.

Dismayed, she asked herself why she should hesitate. It was not from any pity for Ouro Preto. Pity is the only for the weak and Ouro Preto was not weak. Nor did her hesitation arise from sympathy or friendship. Miss Byrd was experienced enough to know that no woman could feel either sympathy or friendship for Ouro Preto except at her peril; besides, she told herself that she did not even like him. His attitude toward her irritated her; and his pride, based on his father's wealth and his mother's ancestry, was as offensive as it was unconscious.

Nor was she ashamed of her work; at least, she had never been so before.

Miss Byrd did not know why she hesitated and the fact that she did hesitate both angered and frightened her.

Ouro Preto did not realize the situation. His admiration for Miss Byrd had begun long before in Berlin and had steadily increased since the day he had come on board the Southern Cross and found her, and had grown intense as the voyage wore on. When the ship reached Barbadoes, at which island he had expected to transfer to his own yacht, which had come from Hamburg to meet him, he had been unable to tear himself away from the fascinating American and had decided to go on to New York on the Southern Cross and sail for Germany from there. Again and again he had striven to place his relations with her on a sentimental footing, but always she evaded him, and the closing days of the voyage found him uncertain as to her feelings and determined to bring matters to a climax. He never guessed that it was on just this that Miss Byrd was counting.

When he reached her chair, he stood over it until he forced her to raise her eyes. Then he bowed. "May I sit down?" he asked.

For a moment the girl did not answer. Then she put out her hand and pushed the chair near her an inch or two farther away. "The chair belongs to the ship and the deck belongs to whomever occupies it," she replied coldly, though her heart was fluttering.

The smile faded from Ouro Preto's face. "Oh! but why are you so cruel," he cried, wildly. "What have I done to anger you? Is it that my love offends you?"

Miss Byrd gasped. "I am not offended at all," she answered briskly, ignoring the suggestion in the young fellow's last words. "I am merely tired—bored if you will—by the length of this never-ending voyage. I am a very bad-tempered young woman, senor; and if you knew me at all well you would realize how unpleasant I am likely to be when I am bored." The girl spoke hurriedly, feeling for words which would not be too rude and which might yet stave off the proposal which she felt was imminent.

But Ouro Preto was not to be stopped. "I do not believe it, senorita," he babbled. "No, I do not believe it. You are altogether sweet and lovely—fit for a duchess. And I can make you one, senorita. Great things are impending. A few weeks more and I will be a duke and—"

His words steadied the girl. "Stop!" she cried. "I will not listen. I am not the inexperienced girl you think me. I am—"

"You are the one woman for me. You do not love me, senorita. I know it. But I can teach you to love me if you will give me the chance. And I can give you much—much. I do not speak of money—no! no! do not think of it! Money is nothing! I can give you more than money. I can give you position, rank, fame."

Miss Byrd forced a laugh. "Where?" she demanded. "In Brazil?"

"In Brazil, yes, at first; then where you will. Listen, senorita, my mother is descended from the princely German house of Hochstein, now extinct in the male line. The emperor is about to revive its honors and vest them in me—in me, do you understand. And this is not all. I am at the head of a great movement. Since I was a boy of sixteen I have been laboring for it, and now at last the time is ripe. Only one obstacle remains, and I am about to sweep it aside. Then—then—"

The man's eyes burned: his breath came hot and fast. His tones carried the intoxication of assured success.

"It is a great game and a great stake," he hurried on. "A great game. Its web involves four continents; it stretches from Brazil across both the Atlantic and the Pacific and far to the northward. And at its center I sit. Strand by strand I have woven it and tested it. It cannot break. Why! see here!"

He thrust his hand into his pocket and drew out a paper, which he tore apart with shaking fingers. "See!" he cried. "See what the emperor has written. With his own hand he has written it! Read! Read!"

The girl pushed away his hand. "No! No!" she cried. "I won't read! I won't listen."

But the man would not be denied. "Read! Read!" he clamored. "Read! See what the emperor promises." Determinedly he thrust the paper before her eyes, and held it there while its words burned themselves into the girl's brain, never to be forgotten.

"You see! You see!" he cried.

Miss Byrd drew back. Her brain was whirling. Half understood facts and unintelligible rumors had suddenly blended into a comprehensive whole. Rutile's fancies had become facts—the facts of a great political conspiracy. It was not merely what Ouro Preto had said; taken alone that might be set down as the vaporings of a dreamer who took wishes and fancies for facts. But dreamers do not receive letters such as his from the Kaiser; and their dreams are not corroborated by a horde of apparently unrelated facts such as Miss Byrd had in her possession.

The man was still speaking. "Only one thing remains in my way now," he triumphed. "Nothing but these cursed Yankees can oppose me. And now I am going to draw their teeth. Too long have they assumed to control the destinies of all the Americans. Too long have they stood in my way. Now— now I am about to eliminate them—to crush them if they dare to interpose. Thank God you are English—"

"But I am not English!"

The man started back. "Not English!" he babbled. "Not English! Are you not the niece of Lord Maxwell?"

"No! I am—I am—Count! I have deceived you. I have let you think me English. I knew you had a secret and I wanted to wheedle it out of you. I am ashamed—ashamed. I don't know why! I never was ashamed of my work before. But I am now. You cannot say anything too bad for me. I deserve it all." The girl bowed her head and her shoulders shook.

The man caught her wrist, and spun her around to face him. "You are a government spy?" he demanded desperately.

The girl shook her head. "No! I am a newspaper woman."

The man's bowed shoulders suddenly straightened. Hope sprang up in him. "A newspaper woman! Then—then—Come! That is not so bad. You can resign and marry me."

But Lillian shook her head. "No! No! I cannot," she murmured. "I am sorry, but—I cannot."

Ouro Preto stared at her. Then: "Well? Let that go for the moment. Later— But now—See? I am rich! very rich! I will pay you two—three years' salary and you will forget all that I have said. It is a bargain? No?"

But the girl bowed her head miserably. "Oh!" she cried. "I have fallen low— low! I said you could say nothing too hard for me to hear, but I never dreamed that you—you of all men—would offer me money! that you should think me for sale. I am shamed. I have had to earn my own living and I have done it. I have gone on from step to step, not realizing. But, believe me, I never did anything quite so indefensible as this before. I never tricked a man's love to get his secret before."

The man was listening intently. But his thoughts were clearly of himself, and not of her. He seemed to have forgotten the words of love that he had breathed only a few moments before. When he spoke his tones still trembled, but with an emotion very different from love.

"Then you will not forget?" he asked.

"How can I?" whispered the girl, miserably. "If I only could! But I can't! I can't. I can resign and I will. I shall give nothing to the paper about you. If your secret were almost anything but what it is, I would repeat it to no one. But"—the girl's figure straightened—"but you are plotting against my country! and I must warn those who should know. I must! I must! You see that, don't you, Count?"

Pleadingly she leaned forward and gazed up into his face.

"You would not have me a traitor, would you?" she questioned, pitifully. "I don't know just what you and your emperor are plotting, but I can guess and I must report it. Why! count, my ancestors have been Americans for nearly three hundred years. They have been soldiers, statesman, patriots! I can't be the first of my line to play the traitor. I can't let the Emperor William plot against my country without warning."

The man forced a laugh. "Plots! Plots! What are you talking about? There is no plot. Only a—a—oh, nothing at all. It is only a—a diplomatic errand to your State Department. Surely it needs no warning against my diplomacy. Plots! Heavens! What sort of a plot could Germany carry through against the United States. Your strenuous President would smash any plot in a moment, even at the cost of war. And do you think Germany wants war? No! No! a thousand times no. It is only a diplomatic triumph that I seek to win. To lose it would discredit me for all time. You do not wish for that! No! No! senorita! Your government needs no help from you. Let it play its own game."

But the girl shook her head. In her mind's eye she saw the web of which Ouro Preto had spoken. Wide and strong it stretched over half the world. Beneath its shadow she could see the flash of cannon and the smoke of ruined cities, with half the world bathed in blood.

The vision faded. Once more she saw the swaying deck, flashing waves, the masts and funnels tracing wide arcs across the blue firmament. Ouro Preto was still speaking; he was asking her something—something that she could not understand. With new eyes she looked upon him. All fascination, all liking, all friendship had vanished. She could see only the enemy with whom she must cope. Blindly she struggled to her feet, pushed past the man's opposing arms and fled away to her stateroom.

That night she sent the long wireless message that McNew showed to the President.

CHAPTER XXIV

Dusk was falling when the torpedo boat Watson turned her nose seaward and sped away from Old Point with all the vigor of her quadruple expansion engines. Topham had climbed on board half a minute before, and full speed ahead had been signalled to the engines as his foot had touched the deck.

Lieutenant Quentin, commander of the Watson, acknowledged his salute with due ceremony. "I have been instructed by telegraph to proceed to sea under your orders the moment you arrive, Mr. Topham," he announced.

Topham bowed. "Very good, Mr. Quentin. Please run to the capes of the Chesapeake, keeping as far south as possible. Have your wireless ready for use as soon as we get outside the bay. Meanwhile I will go over the charts with you and lay a course."

Down in the cabin he bent over a chart spread upon the table, and punched a small hole in it with the point of his pencil.

"The Southern Cross was here at 10 last night," he said. "She was bound for New York, and was running presumably about twelve knots an hour." He ruled a pencil line on the map and scaled off 220 miles along it. "She should be about here?" he decided, "at nine tonight. Twenty miles an hour would bring us to the same point at about the same hour. Therefore, Mr. Quentin, please make your course east-southeast, nothing south, as soon as we get to the capes."

Quentin nodded and gave the orders. "Anything else, sir?" he questioned.

"Not just yet. Our errand is to find the Southern Cross and bring ashore one of her passengers. So, in good time, you can give orders to try to raise her by wireless. That's about the only way outside of plain bull beck that we could possibly locate her tonight."

"Right you are!" Ceremony was satisfied, and Quentin relaxed. "Say, Walter," he exclaimed, "the Secretary must be in a horrible hurry to reach her. She'd be in New York day after tomorrow."

"It's the President and not the Secretary, and he is in a hurry indeed. I'm not at liberty to tell you why. The passenger—a lady—sent a wireless ashore last night, and the message reached the President this morning. The whole affair is to be kept a strict secret."

"Of course. The lady'll be expecting us, then?"

"I think not. I'm pretty sure not. But she'll be glad to come, I think. She's a newspaper woman—a Miss Lillian Byrd. You know her, don't you?"

"Know her! I should say I did. Wasn't I sweet on her once. Why! You old hypocrite, you know her yourself. By Jove! I'm remembering! You were the hardest hit of all the fellows—"

But Topham shook his head. "No! that's over long ago," he answered, soberly. "She turned me down very hard, and I—well, I've gotten over it. This isn't a question of romance, you know. It's serious—more serious than I can tell you."

The torpedo boat heeled far over; then rolled back again. Quentin rose. "We've reached the capes, evidently," he remarked. "I'll go to the deck and take charge." He glanced at the chart. "East-southeast a little east!" he repeated. "Make yourself comfortable, old man. I'll notify you if anything turns up, or if the wireless man catches anything."

But Topham shook his head. "No! I'll come on deck, too," he said.

Steadily the Watson thrashed eastward into the deepening night, not rising on the waves but cutting through them and getting the full benefit of their differential lift. Steadily, too, the wireless operator sent his call across the waters.

It was two hours before he got an answer. Then, as ordered, he sent word to Topham, and the latter hurried to his side.

"I've got the Southern Cross," he announced.

"Good! Tell him who we are. Have him notify the captain that I wish to come aboard him, and ask for his position and course and speed."

The operator's fingers played over the key—the ridiculously exaggerated key of the wireless. Soon he stopped and noted the reply upon a blank sheet of paper.

Topham called a messenger and sent the note to Quentin, asking him to lay his course accordingly. Then he turned back to the wireless operator.

"Ask him whether Miss Lillian Byrd is on board?" he said.

Promptly came an affirmative answer.

"Please tell her that Commander Topham of the Navy will be alongside in about half an hour to take her ashore, and ask her to be ready for transfer. Tell the captain that Mr. Topham apologizes for the trouble he is giving, but that the matter is imperative."

The operator tapped off the message. "The operator has gone to deliver them, sir," he explained. "He'll call again in a few minutes."

But more than a few minutes chased themselves across the clock's face before the Southern Cross again made herself heard. In fact, the "Light! Ho!" of the lookout at the bow of the Watson was sounding before her call came again.

For an instant the operator listened; then he snatched up his pencil and began to write. Topham, looking over his shoulder, read the words.

"Miss Byrd cannot be found. Was on board at nine o'clock. Count of Ouro Preto, another passenger, has also vanished. No trace of either found."

"Good God! Ask him if they have no idea what has become of them!"

Again the operator wrote: "No trace of either can be found, but we suspect Ouro Preto carried girl off. His yacht has been following us all the way from Barbadoes. He sent a code wireless to it last night. Saw her lights very close behind us an hour ago."

In silent consternation Topham read the message. It confirmed his instant guess as to what had happened. To keep his secret Ouro Preto had snatched the girl from under the President's very fingers. Just how he had managed it was not of import, except as concerned the welfare of the girl herself; and Topham was very sure by now that more important things were at stake than the fate even of Lillian Byrd.

What should he do? What should he do?

What could he do? In what quarter of the sea should he seek for the fleeing yacht?

Suddenly the operator began to write again. "Somebody's breaking in," he explained. "Not the Southern Cross; somebody else." His fingers raced over the paper.

"Heard you talking," ran the message. "This is the yacht Windbird. Ouro Preto just came aboard bringing Miss Byrd with him. We are due south of Southern Cross, going east. Will try to keep you advised. Can't say much, or I may excite suspicion. Follow.—Rutile."

CHAPTER XXV

When Rutile ran down to Hamburg to see what he could learn about the gun-running expeditions that Lillian Byrd had warned him were leaving that port he had nothing in mind beyond making a few inquiries which, if it seemed best, he might tip off to the Brazilian government. Circumstances, however, played into his hands and led him into a far more extensive adventure than he had foreseen.

In early life Rutile had intended to be a sailor. He had been appointed a cadet at the naval academy at Annapolis and had gone through the full four years course there and the requisite two succeeding years of sea service. If Uncle Sam had been willing he would have remained in the navy. But in those days Uncle Sam had no navy worth speaking about, and every year he deliberately turned adrift about two-thirds of the gallant young fellows whom he had been training for six years. Only about a score of each class graduated received commissions. Rutile was one of those dropped with a year's pay.

Balked in following his chosen profession the young fellow had gone in for diplomacy. But he had never lost his fondness for the sea, and being blessed (or cursed) with abundance of money, had continued to keep in touch with sea life and to spend a month or more afloat every year. His father had been German born and he himself had been familiar with the language from childhood. He was thus qualified for the task he had set himself.

Arrived at Hamburg his first move was to take lodgings in a cheap quarter of the town and there to slip into such clothes as a petty ship's officer would be likely to wear. These donned, he went out and wandered along the water front, chatting with sailors and pretending to be on the lookout for a berth as wireless operator, a calling that he had chosen chiefly because he was very certain that no ship's captain was likely to put his good faith to the test by offering him a job. Incidentally he kept his ears open for news of the filibusters.

To a certain extent his task proved surprisingly simple. A few drinks and a few hours loafing told him that Miss Byrd's suspicions were well-founded. The munitions of war supplied to the rebels in Southern Brazil had been shipped from Hamburg, practically without concealment, a few months before. He learned, moreover, that three or four ships supposed to be similarly laden had recently sailed for South American ports; "and yonder," continued his informant, pointing with the stem of his pipe; "yonder lies the flagship. They say she'll be sailing soon."

Rutile needed no second glance to identify the vessel indicated. She was Ouro Preto's yacht, which he had often seen. Nevertheless, he loafed out upon the docks for a nearer view.

Work was being knocked off for the day as he strolled to the end of the stone pier and stared across the dirty water to where the yacht was lying. He noticed that she had steam up, and guessed that his informant was right, and that she intended to leave very soon indeed. As he watched he saw a steam launch leave her side and come puffing toward the shore.

Dusk was falling fast, and at last he turned away, feeling that he had accomplished all that he had come down to do.

He knew that it was no use to try to stop the yacht's sailing; the very openness with which the thing had been carried on was proof of the connivance of the authorities. His best, and indeed his only course was to hurry back to Berlin and notify both the United States and Brazilian governments.

He was about to step off the pier when he saw two men coming toward him. One of them he recognized as the man with whom he had been talking not long before. As they drew near this man jerked his head in his direction and spoke to the other.

"That's him," he said. Rutile heard the words distinctly.

The second man, who was clearly an officer of some sort, changed his course slightly, and stopped just in front of the American.

"I understand you are looking for a berth as wireless operator," he said gruffly, in German.

Rutile concealed his astonishment as well as he could. "I am," he answered, promptly, in the same tongue.

"Good." The officer turned to the man who accompanied him, and handed him a coin. "All right!" he said. "Be off."

Then he swung back to Rutile. "My name's Caspar," he said. "I'm second mate of the yacht Windbird. That's her yonder." He indicated Ouro Preto's yacht. "Our operator took suddenly ill and I just brought him ashore." Rutile remembered the launch he had seen leaving the yacht. "We're sailing in an hour and want an operator in a hurry and the Marconi people can't supply us in less than twenty-four hours. If you're sure you're qualified and would like the berth you can have it."

Before the man had half finished Rutile had seen what was coming and had done some rapid thinking. Mad as he admitted his acceptance of the proposition would be, it nevertheless tempted him strongly. He was an adventurous fellow, was Rutile; and the danger of the thing appealed to him.

As wireless operator he must necessarily be trusted to an extent that would give him a chance to find out something really valuable about what he had come to believe was a great political conspiracy. On the other hand, it was a good deal easier to get into such an adventure than it would be to get out of it. And what would the Ambassador say?

These thoughts flashed like lightning through his mind, but did not mirror themselves in his face. He had not been in diplomatic training for nothing. When the mate stopped he was ready to answer.

"I'll take it," he declared.

"Good! Can you come now?"

"Now?" Events were moving too quick even for Rutile's hasty nature.

"Yes!" impatiently. "It's now or not at all. I told you we sailed within an hour."

Rutile shook his head. "I've got to have half an hour," he declared positively. "I've got a room near here and I've got to pay for it and get my dunnage. But I'll be ready in half an hour."

The mate hesitated. "I suppose that's got to do," he acquiesced at last. "Yonder's the launch. I'll wait for you half an hour and not a minute longer. Hurry."

Rutile hurried, and was back within the time allowed. He had spent half of it in talking with the Ambassador over the long-distance telephone, and most of the other half in buying an outfit for the trip.

"I'm taking you on trust," observed the mate, as the launch puffed toward the Windbird. "But the old man won't. He trusts nobody. If you're not qualified you'd better say so now. It isn't quite so long a swim ashore from here."

Rutile grinned. "Oh! I'm qualified," he insisted. "What system have you?"

"Marconi!"

"That's all right. I understand it perfectly. You'll remember that I'm taking a good deal on trust, too. Where are we bound?"

"Barbadoes first. Afterwards—who knows? We're going down to meet the owner and then we'll go where he says."

"Humph!" Rutile considered. "I guess I'll only sign for Barbadoes," he declared. "By the time we get there I'll know whether I care to stay or not."

CHAPTER XXVI

Lillian Byrd kept in her cabin most of the day after she sent her dispatch to the Gazette, leaving it only for meals and slipping back to it the moment these were finished. Although she had done only what she had felt to be her duty, she yet shrank from facing Ouro Preto and confessing her action.

She knew that he would not consider her last words final, but would urge her to change them; and it was largely the fear that she might not be as steadfast as she wanted to be that led her to send the dispatch giving McNew the information that she had gained and urging him to lay it before the President of the country. She felt that the count had a powerful influence over her, and that she could be sure of herself only when it was out of her power to accede to his wishes. Later she felt really afraid to face him.

Face him she must sooner or later, however. Even if he remained quiescent she could not well seclude herself for the remainder of the trip; and few things seemed to be more certain than that he would not remain quiescent. He would insist on seeing her; the fact that he left her in peace for twenty-four hours merely showed either that he was content to let her consider matters quietly, or that he, too, was uncertain as to what was to be done.

Lillian was not ordinarily a coward, and after a day's reflection the situation grew intolerable to her, and she determined to give the count an opportunity to bring matters to a focus. Bitter as his reproaches might be, they could not be worse than the anticipation of them. She would face him and bear his words as best she might.

Evening therefore saw her upon the deck in the self-same spot where he had found her the evening before—waiting.

She waited long! Daylight waned and vanished. The crescent moon flashed out for an hour and then followed the sun below the horizon, leaving the big stars as sole lights in the firmament. She looked aft across the water to where the three lights of Ouro Preto's yacht had burned night after night, and noted that they were closer than she had ever seen them before. Little by little the decks had grown empty as the passengers had slipped away to more congenial occupations than watching the white boiling spume of the wake and listening to the swish of the waves along the steamer's sides. One or two soft-footed figures—stewards or sailors engaged in ships tasks—moved ghost-like beneath the awnings, but if any others were still on deck they were hidden in the shadows. For all that Lillian could see she was alone.

Four bells struck and still the count had not come. Lillian did not know whether to be glad or angry. On the one hand she was relieved to be spared what he might say; on the other she was woman enough to resent his neglect, as if he had found her further actions or words unimportant. When he did come at last she was in the mood for combat rather than apology.

He bowed as he came up, and wished her a good-evening. Then for a few moments he stood looking down at her in silence, not as if hesitating as to what he was to say, but rather as one acting in accordance with some set plan.

"I have come for my answer," he said, at last, with a tremor in his voice. "Will you give it to me?"

"Your answer?" Amazement drove all other emotion from Lillian's mind. Not thus had she expected Ouro Preto to address her.

"Yes!" Surprise, real or pretended, sounded in the Brazilian's tones. "But, yes! I asked you to marry me last night and you ran away without answering. Ah! Senorita. You do not know what this day has been to me! One moment I hope! the next I despair. I love you, senorita. Will you not say that you too love me!"

Lillian's thoughts whirled, aimless as the spray from the steamer's bow. "But—but—" she gasped. "The Emperor! Your great plot! You—All of it."

Ouro Preto stared. Then he laughed gently. "Por Dios! senorita!" he cried. "Have you not forgotten that—that bombast?"

"Bombast?"

"But yes!" He waved his hand airily. "Nothing more! Waste no more thought over it. It is gone! But you remain—you and I! Will you not think of my suit. Ah! Senorita! If you but understand how I love you!"

But Lillian shook her head. "I can not forget it," she declared, stubbornly, refusing to be diverted. "I cannot forget it. I wish I could. I am ashamed that I should have imposed upon you as I did. I wish that you had not told me but now that you have done so, I cannot forget and I cannot keep it secret. In fact, I must tell you that I have already—"

The count flung up his hand. "No! No! Think once more, senorita," he pleaded.

"I can not. I have—"

"Then, senorita, I must take other measures. I have given you every chance, and you have refused. Now—Now!"

The man did not even raise his voice. In exactly the same tones as those he had been using, he repeated his last word "Now!"

Vaguely uneasy; fearing she knew not what, Lillian started to rise. But before she could do so, a towel saturated with some heavy-smelling stuff, was flung over her face from behind, and her head was drawn suddenly back. Vainly she tried to scream; the muffling towel was too thick. She gasped for breath, plucking with futile fingers at the bandage. Then her brain reeled; and darkness came over her.

Ouro Preto stood silently, quietly watching her struggles. When at last she lay still he spoke in a low tone to the sailor who held her.

"Loosen the towel a little and give her air," he ordered. "I don't want to suffocate her."

As the man obeyed the count stepped to the taffrail, and stared back to where the lights of his yacht gleamed through the darkness. After a moment he lifted the rear light of the steamer from its box, and swung it in wide wagon wheel convolutions—swung it until from out of the waters behind him a white sword of light sprang up and cleft the zenith. Right and left it wheeled, cutting fantastic zigzags across the milky way, but never by any chance falling upon the Southern Cross.

His yacht had hung on the heels of the Southern Cross all the way from Barbadoes, until those upon the steamer had ceased to pay attention to her. On that particular night she had closed in until scarcely an eighth of a mile of smooth rolling water separated the two vessels. When the search light sprang up, the officers on the Southern Cross watched it for a moment and then turned to more important things, neither noting nor caring that the yacht was rapidly eating up the distance that had separated her from them.

Meanwhile Ouro Preto was busy. From a rack above his head he took two life preservers; one he bound around himself, and the other he handed to his confederate to fasten around Miss Byrd's unconscious form.

"Come along," he ordered, turning to the starboard quarter, whence a trailing rope ladder—a so-called Jacob's ladder—depended, its lower end just touching the crests of the waves as they rolled past.

He climbed over the rail and took a step or two down the swaying ladder. "Give me the girl," he ordered.

But the man held back. "Say, Mister," he protested. "I ain't standing for no murder."

Ouro Preto glared at him. "Neither am I, you fool," he snarled. "It's all arranged. I can swim like a fish, and my yacht will pick us up in less than five minutes. See how near she is."

The man looked up. The yacht was indeed very near.

"Give me the girl," ordered the count, again, and this time the sailor obeyed.

Ouro Preto balanced Lillian over his shoulder and descended the Jack ladder step by step. When he reached the water's edge he stopped.

"Swing the light around your head twice," he called, softly.

The sailor obeyed and instantly the yacht's searchlight crept along the water until it rested with sudden brilliancy on the stern of the Southern Cross and on Ouro Preto where he clung to the Jacob's ladder with Lillian in his arms.

For only an instant he clung; then he descended the last two or three steps of the ladder and when the next wave came let go his hold and dropped upon its crest.

The fall carried the two beneath the surface, but the life preservers brought them up again as quickly as a bobbing cork. In the interval, brief as it was, the Southern Cross had drawn away; the count could see her stern light rapidly lessening in the distance. The yacht's searchlight came and went, sweeping over him often enough to prevent his being lost in the waters, but not often enough to attract belated attention from the Southern Cross.

Then Lillian revived, drawn back to life by the shock of the chill water. Half conscious, bewildered, terror stricken, she struggled desperately to free herself from the count and he let her go for an instant only to grasp hold of her life belt again as a wave tried to force them apart.

"It's all right, Miss Byrd," he declared. "It's all right. Don't be frightened."

But Lillian would not heed. "Help! Help!" she screamed across the water.

Ouro Preto made no effort to check her. "It is of no use, senorita," he declared, simply. "The Southern Cross is half a mile away and cannot hear you."

Miss Byrd gripped at her sinking courage. She realized that she was not drowning, and she tried desperately to calm herself. "How dare you?" she choked. "How dare you?"

The count shrugged his shoulders. "I was forced," he explained. "I could not let you wreck the plan of years. Believe me, senorita, it grieves me to the heart to use such means as these. I love you and—"

"Love!"

"Yes! Love! You may not believe it. I cannot blame you if you do not, but it is true. And, senorita, have no fear. We will be on my yacht in a few minutes;

and you will be as safe there as you were on the Southern Cross. I will release you very soon—as soon as safety will allow—probably within two weeks. But I cannot permit the knowledge of my plans to reach Washington just now!"

Lillian was no longer frightened. The circling searchlight flashed across her face, and very close at hand she heard the noise of oars in rowlocks. Besides she was choking with rage, and rage had driven out fear.

It was on the tip of her tongue to tell the count that his action was vain; that his plans had already been wirelessed to land and had very probably already been printed broadcast. How she could exult over him! But on second thoughts she held her tongue. She knew instinctively that he would not under any circumstances restore her to the steamer from which he had taken her. Perhaps he could not do so even if he would, and she felt sure that he would not if he could.

When the Southern Cross reached port, she would be looked for, and her and his disappearance would be understood, and steps would be taken for her rescue. To tell him would merely be to warn him and cause him to take precautions that might lessen her chances of early freedom.

Besides, now that the thing was done, she was beginning to feel that it might all be for the best. She no longer felt the least regret over her own action. The fact that the count had gone to the lengths he did to seal her lips proved that something of great moment was afoot. Her disappearance would add more force to the warning she had sent than would anything she could say. And here she was forcibly forked into the very focus of the conspiracy where, if anywhere, she would have an opportunity to learn all about its tangled threads. And if she learned anything she would no longer hesitate to use it. Since Ouro Preto had resorted to open war, she could fight back with good grace. For herself she had no fear. She did not believe that he would dare to harm her. On the whole, she began to feel rather glad that she had been kidnapped.

Ouro Preto had been watching her in silence. "Well?" he questioned.

Lillian shrugged her shoulders. "Well!" she replied definitively. "Since I can't help myself, I yield for the time being. But I warn you that you will have to pay some day."

The count leaned forward. "I am ready to pay now," he cried eagerly; "to pay with all I have. Marry me, and—"

"No thank you! Change the subject, please! How did you get me away from the steamer?"

Ouro Preto spread out his hands. "Very easily," he explained. "I carry much gold. The man on watch at the steamer's quarter wanted it, and so—Oh! It was easy. But"—he looked up—"But, senorita, here is the Windbird. The men will lift you on board."

At full speed the boat came slopping alongside. Two of the sailors dropped their oars and dragged the girl into the boat, and an instant later Ouro Preto clambered in beside her. Two minutes later both were on board the Windbird.

As Lillian, dripped and bedraggled but unconquered, went to her cabin, she and the wireless operator met face to face. For one breathless instant she hesitated; then Rutile lifted his cap and stepped aside.

"Pardon, fraulein," he said.

Miss Byrd bowed in acknowledgment. "On guard!" she whispered.

CHAPTER XXVII

Through the night, full speed, with all lights extinguished, ran the Watson, her only guide the information contained in Rutile's brief and indefinite message over the wireless. If this were correct—if the yacht had indeed run due east for half an hour and if she should continue in the same direction and at the same speed, and if her speed were about 18 knots an hour (as it probably was), it was a mere matter of calculation to determine where and when the Watson would overtake her.

But there were many "ifs" in these premises. The night was dark; the moon had set hours before, and the stars were invisible behind a light film of clouds. If the Windbird should run without lights, as she certainly would if Ouro Preto should suspect pursuit (and as she might in any case), she would be invisible even at close range, unless betrayed by the glow from her funnels. To find her without further help from Rutile would be like seeking a needle in the darkest sort of a haystack. Even with Rutile's aid, Topham felt that he had no right to hope to find her while night lasted. He did hope, however, to hang so closely on her heels that her smoke should be visible above the horizon when morning dawned.

Swiftly the moments sped by, and steadily the destroyer ate up the miles supposed to intervene between her and the yacht. No further signals came, and Topham, not knowing what conditions might be on the Windbird or who might read off any message that he might send flying through the dark, forebore to call, despite Quentin's advice to take the chance.

He yielded only when the Watson had reached the spot where calculation placed the Windbird.

"I guess you'd better call Rutile, Mr. Quentin," he ordered. "We'll be passing the yacht the first thing we know."

Quentin was about to give the order when the operator suddenly began to write.

"Do you hear me?" he scribbled, as the words come through the night. "Answer if you do."

"I hear," tapped the operator.

"Am using reduced power. Been ordered to call H. I. M. Kaiserland, supposed to be somewhere near. Can see light from somebody's funnels and suspect it's yours or hers. If it's yours you're due north of us, mighty near."

Topham leaped for the companionway. "South by east, Mr. Quentin," he ordered. "Half speed. Keep sharp lookout! We're close on her."

"Tell him that," he ordered, turning back to the operator.

"Good!" Came the answer. "You don't want the Kaiserland to beat you to it. She's an armored cruiser."

Quentin bent over the cabin skylight. "Saw her funnels flash just now," he cried, excitedly. "How about the searchlight?"

"Turn it on."

Topham leaped on deck. As he did so the broad white sword of the searchlight flashed through the darkness, lighting up the rolling water and picking out the Windbird black against the night, scarce a cable length away. The blinding light showed her every detail—showed her masts and funnels and the white tracery of her rigging, silvered the edges of the black smoke that trailed away behind her, and showed, too, her half dozen rapid fire guns, with their crews manned and ready.

"Hail them. Say you'll send a boat," ordered Topham.

Quentin flung up his megaphone. "Windbird ahoy," he bellowed. "Heave to. I'll send a boat aboard you."

As the words left his lips the Windbird's searchlight flashed out and lighted up the bulk of the torpedo boat, long and low, far less formidable to all appearances than the yacht.

A man on the yacht's bridge raised a megaphone. "Who are you?" he demanded.

"That's Ouro Preto talking," commented Topham, staring through his glasses.

"The United States Destroyer Watson. Heave to!" ordered Quentin.

"Go to hell!"

Topham's face flushed. You cannot tell an officer of the United States Navy to go to hell without consequences. Fortunately the young fellow was not impulsive. "Easy, Mr. Quentin," he cautioned. "Warn him once more."

"For the last time, heave to, you damned pirate," shouted Quentin. "Heave to! or I'll fire into you."

Back came the answer. "Fire if you dare!"

Quentin lowered the megaphone. His eyes glittered and his breast swelled with unholy joy. "It's up to us," he suggested.

"Send a shot between his masts," ordered Topham. "It may bring him to his senses."

"Crack." The spiteful snap of the aft six-pounder thrilled through the night, and Topham saw the men on the yacht duck as the projectile whistled about their heads.

The next instant Ouro Preto's voice, crazy with rage rose. "Fire! Fire!" he yelled.

But the yachtsmen did not fire. Ready as most of them were to take the risks of battle with the Brazilian government, they were not ready to fire upon a United States ship. Small though it might be, it carried the power and dignity of the nation.

They did not fire, but still the yacht swept on. "I'll put the next shot through your pilot house," megaphoned Quentin. "Be warned!" "Train on the pilot house," he ordered, in tones loud enough to reach the yacht.

"Ay! Ay! Sir!" The gunners bent to their piece, but before they could fire the door of the pilot house of the Seabird flew open and a man, ducking low, ran out. Instantly the yacht, uncontrolled, swung off into the trough of the waves.

"You damned cowards!" Ouro Preto's voice was unintelligible with rage. He snatched up a rifle and flung it to his shoulder, but some one knocked up his arm and the bullet whistled harmlessly over Topham's head.

As the sound lost itself in the immensity of the ocean, Quentin's voice sounded. "Heave to!" he ordered, calmly.

The clang of the engine bells answered and the yacht lost way. Instantly the Watson followed suit, sheering inward as she did so. Closer they came and closer until the Watson poked her sharp nose under the yacht's overhanging counter, and Topham caught the trailing Jacob ladder and swarmed over the rail and dropped upon her deck.

Ouro Preto faced him. "What does this—this piracy mean?" he demanded.

Topham took no notice of the words. He could afford to ignore them. Besides Ouro Preto was "her" brother. Politely he saluted.

"I am instructed by the President of the United States to bring him the young lady whom you kidnapped tonight. Kindly produce her!"

"I won't do it."

Topham shrugged his shoulders. "Then I shall be compelled to take you into port as a pirate," he said, distinctly.

Ouro Preto shook with the fury that possessed him. The hopes of years were crumbling before his eyes.

"You have no right," he clamored. "No right. This is a German vessel—"

"Your pardon. She was once a Brazilian ship, but she has forfeited her rights by engaging in rebellion against Brazil. She is now an outlaw if not a pirate. Give up the girl and do not force me to take the vessel of a former friend into port as a prize."

Ouro Preto glared for a moment. But before he could utter the defiance that was on the end of his tongue, a feminine voice broke in.

"Good-evening, Mr. Topham!" it said, sweetly. "You've come in good time." Lillian Byrd stood smilingly by, with Rutile beside her. As all eyes were turned on her. She went on. "Mr. Rutile let me out of the stateroom where the count had locked me. You didn't know Mr. Rutile was on board, did you, Count?"

Helplessly Ouro Preto stared from one to the other. "Rutile!" he gasped. "You here?"

Rutile nodded. "Sure thing," he remarked, genially. "Been on board for three weeks. Wireless operator, you know. Sorry, but the game's up, old man. It is, really!"

"One moment!" A man whom no one had seen before stepped quickly into the middle of the group. Behind him stood half a dozen sailors.

Gravely he saluted. "Whom have I the honor of addressing?" he demanded, looking at Topham.

Topham returned the salute. "I am Commander Topham, of the United States Navy," he answered, taking in the newcomer's uniform as he did so. "And you, mein Herr."

"I am Commander Metternich, of His Imperial Majesty's ship Kaiserland. Captain Vreeland of the Kaiserland learned, through intercepted wireless messages, that the operator on this ship is a traitor. He therefore hastened here and sent me on board to demand his surrender. No one seemed to observe my arrival and I took the liberty of listening for a moment. What I have heard convinces me that the case is not so simple as I thought. I therefore take possession of this ship as a prize of His Imperial Majesty. The Kaiserland will escort her to Hamburg. If you so desire, sir, you may accompany her."

Before the last word had fallen from the German's lips, Topham stepped between him and Rutile. "Look sharp," he hissed to the American. Then, facing the German, he flung out his hand. "I'm delighted to hear you, commander," he declared! "Frankly, I didn't know what to do with the yacht, which is clearly little better than a pirate, but your action solves everything. I can't tell you how much I thank you."

As he spoke, Topham pressed forward, crowding Metternich backward, apparently merely by excess enthusiasm. The latter gave way for a moment, though clearly bewildered by the American's sudden excess of friendliness.

Suddenly a warning cry rang out. "Stop them! Quick!" yelled Ouro Preto. "He's fooling you. He's fooling you!"

The Brazilian was right. As Topham grasped the officer's hand Rutile caught Lillian by the arm and darted with her toward the rail, only half a dozen feet away, beyond which lay the Watson. The German sailors sprang to intercept them, but Rutile, leaving Lillian to scramble over by herself, turned at bay and struck out savagely twice. Then, before he could be grasped, he vaulted over the side of the deck of the Watson.

Metternich saw it all over Topham's shoulder, and with a cry of rage, he tried to jerk free from the American's grasp. But Topham laughed and chattered on for a moment longer. Then releasing the man he sprang back to the rail.

The crew of the Watson, arms in hand, were swarming up the sides to his rescue, but he waved them back. One of the German sailors was about to spring down, and him Topham caught by the shoulders and flung aside. Then he threw up his hand.

"Stop!" he thundered.

A pause followed, brief but sufficient. Topham did not let it slip.

"Call back your men, commander," he ordered, sternly. "Are you mad?"

The German hesitated. Wild with rage as he was at the trick that had been played upon him, he was not so frantic as not to realize the consequences of forcibly boarding a warship of a friendly nation. To do so would mean war; or if the Emperor did not want war, it would mean disgrace for himself. He was only a subordinate, though an able one, and he had no reason to suppose that Wilhelm did want war. Besides, his force, though perhaps sufficient to prevent an escape was clearly not enough for a recapture. Finally he sheathed the sword he had drawn. "You will wait here till I consult Captain Vreeland," he declared positively.

But Topham only laughed. "Your pardon, Commander," he said. "I have been delayed too long already. Take your prize into port if you will. I will content myself with taking the chief witness. Good-night."

Courteously he lifted his cap; then, turning, he climbed slowly over the side of the yacht down to the deck of the Watson.

As he went, Metternich caught up a megaphone and bellowed a torrent of guttural German across the waters toward the Kaiserland. Topham did not hear the answer that came back, for the moment he had touched the deck of the Watson she glided away into the night.

CHAPTER XXVIII

When the night had swallowed up both the yacht and the cruiser, Topham drew a long breath and turned to Lillian.

"Great Scott!" he exclaimed boyishly, "what a yarn this would make for the Gazette—if you could only print it."

Lillian bubbled toward him. "Mayn't I?" she asked, plaintively, but as one who knew the answer already.

But Topham laughed. "Not a word," he said. "The situation is too ticklish. Do you know, young woman, that your respected chief, Mr. McNew, thought it so serious that he brought your dispatch to Washington and showed it to the President without publishing it—to the President, mind you! Your chief and the President! It took something mighty serious to bring those two together. Do you know that the United States and Germany were on the brink of war tonight?"

Lillian nodded. "I suppose so," she answered, seriously, "I suppose, too, that that German officer—Commander Metternich was he?—will have trouble over letting us get away."

Topham nodded, but before he could speak Rutile struck in. "No," he said, "I think not. His captain may give him a wigging, but it's nothing to what the Kaiser would have done to him if he had gone a little too far. Wilhelm doesn't want war. He's merely bluffing."

"But"—Topham was amazed. "But he—"

"Yes! I know. But things are not just as you would suppose. I've had nearly a month's time and first-class opportunities to learn the ins and outs of the whole conspiracy. If we can go below and sit down, I'll try to explain just what I think Wilhelm was after."

In a few minutes the party was sitting around the table in Quentin's cabin. Rutile leaned across it.

"I don't need to point out," he began, "that Germany wants colonies and would prefer southern Brazil if she can get it. Nor do I need to do more than call attention to the fact that Germany is building dreadnoughts supposedly to make her equal to England, but that they really make her much more nearly a rival to the United States. She is also—but I haven't heard any very recent news—Is she by any chance intriguing in Japan?"

"She is," replied Topham, grimly.

"I suspected so. Well! Here's the situation. Wilhelm wants Brazil. Ouro Preto, half a German and son of the richest and most influential man in southern Brazil, wants a German dukedom. Wilhelm says all right; earn it if you want it. Go back to Brazil. Start something in the three southern states. I will help you with arms and officers and munitions. Make good and I'll recognize their independence. Then let them ask me to annex them. You've got 2,000,000 Germans down there. They won't object. Do this and you'll get your dukedom."

Miss Byrd nodded. "That's about true," she confirmed. "The count showed me a letter from the Emperor saying that when south Brazil became a German colony he would make Ouro Preto the Duke of Hochstein."

"But," objected Topham. "The Monroe doctrine—"

"Tush! Tush! The Monroe doctrine is to protect American republics against European conquest. What's it got to do with voluntary annexations?"

Topham knitted his brows. "Of course you are right," he said didactically, "as to the original meaning of the Monroe doctrine. But the meaning has changed. Today it is analogous to the 'balance of power' in Europe, to maintain which so many wars have been fought. Whatever our motives in establishing it, we support it now as a measure of protection to ourselves. If we permit one European country to acquire land over here, others will crowd in and our geographical isolation—an isolation that saves us from the military terrors and burdens of Europe—will be at an end. For our own sakes we must keep Europe away from our doors. I judge the doctrine would be held to apply."

"You *judge*!" Rutile snorted "Pish!! Likewise tush! You *judge*! You are not by any means certain, but after splitting a few hairs you *judge* it would apply! Well, how do you suppose twenty or thirty million German-Americans would judge?"

"Why! They—"

"I'm not saying anything against German-Americans; I'm one of them myself in the second degree. If it comes to fighting, they'll fight, even against the fatherland. But they won't want to fight Germany. They're mighty apt to say 'Mein Gott! Vas ist loss mit der Dagoes that we should go to war for them, ain't it?' And if the German-Americans did want to fight, what would the rich man say—the fellows who have got trade to lose? Don't you know they'd say 'To hades with Brazil; we sell more to Germany in a minute than we do to Brazil in a year!' And so it would go. When it came down to a count of noses, you'd find about the only people that wanted to fight to keep the new republic down in south Brazil from following their God-twisted noses into the German fold would be you navy fellows and a few chaps whom the papers would call jingoes. And if Germany had a fleet as powerful as the United States, and if the United States had other foreign complications on its hands—with Japan if you like—how many people would insist on fighting to save a lot of greasers who didn't want to be saved. Now, do you begin to see?"

Topham nodded. The logic of the situation was too strong for him. Rutile's words brought into vivid consonance all the scattered facts that he himself had noted. He was beginning to understand, as Europe had understood long before, that the warlord of Germany was the most wonderful diplomat the world had known for a century—one who knew how to mask the cunning of a Machiavelli beneath the bluffness of a soldier and the reckless speech of a boy. His was not the iron hand in the velvet glove. With him glove was iron, but the hand was not in it; it was outside, pulling the strings that made the puppets dance.

Topham saw it all. Yet he ventured one more objection, not because he put much faith in it, but because he wanted to hear Rutile's answer.

"But," he said, "suppose the people of the new republics should not want to be annexed," he began. "Suppose they wanted to remain independent—"

"Bosh! Much the people would have to say about it! The leaders would decide, and by the time the people woke up, Germany would be in possession. Wilhelm has got the leaders, body and soul; you can bet on that. This isn't the first time he's tried it, you know. It was all framed up ten or fifteen years ago when the Mello rebellion came off. Germany was behind the rebels then, and Washington knew it. Didn't the President rush a fleet down to Rio, and didn't Admiral Benham smash the rebellion when he found the Brazilian government couldn't do it?"

"Oh! I know he didn't profess to do so. I know he only stood up for American rights and all that. But he smashed it all the same, and not a minute too soon either. And Germany didn't have any dreadnoughts in those days, and she wasn't more than middling anxious for colonies either. It's different today!"

"And Japan!"

"Japan! What does Germany care about Japan? It could fight or funk as it pleased when the time came, if only it would make faces until Germany got settled in South America. There's more ways of getting chestnuts out of the fire than burning your own fingers—and Wilhelm knows every one of them."

"But what is to be done?"

"Done! Smash the rebellion in Brazil before Wilhelm can recognize it. Send a fleet to aid Brazil to blockade her southern coast and cut off the supplies that Germany is sending. Do? Well! That isn't your part nor mine. Our part was to get information. We've got it. The President will do the rest. It's up to him now."

CHAPTER XXIX

At eleven o'clock the next morning Topham, Rutile and Miss Byrd were ushered into the presence of the President. No train had been convenient, and the Watson had brought them all the way to Washington. Her coming had been wired, ahead, and an automobile had been in waiting to rush them to the White House.

One by one the President heard their stories, his square jaw growing squarer and squarer as he listened. Now and then he asked a question, sharp and pertinent, but for the most part he kept silence—a sure proof that he regarded the case as very serious.

When at last the stories had been finished, he nodded. "Between you," he said, "you seem to have gotten the thing down pretty fine. What you have told me today confirms what I felt sure of yesterday after I had heard the story of Commander Topham brought from San Francisco and had read the dispatch Miss Byrd sent from the Southern Cross. Mr. Rutile's information welds it all and makes its inferences unmistakable. Now that I know, I can checkmate my great and good friend across the water. In fact, I have checkmated him already."

The President turned to his secretary. "Have you a copy of today's New York Gazette?" he asked.

The secretary handed him a paper, and he reached it out to Topham. "You heard me promise Mr. McNew a scoop yesterday, Mr. Topham," he remarked. "So I called in his correspondent last night and gave him this. It was quite widely printed this morning. Read it aloud, please! I suppose none of you have seen the papers."

Topham read:

"It is officially announced that the President has decided to send the entire Atlantic fleet on a cruise to the Pacific coast. Sixteen battle ships will leave Hampton Roads in a few weeks and will steam southward around Cape Horn to San Francisco. They will probably make an extended stop at Rio Janeiro and other parts in Brazil. It is hoped and believed that the present rebellion in southern Brazil will be at an end by the time the fleet reaches there. Three vessels of the present south Atlantic squadron will cruise along the coast of south Brazil until the fleet arrives, when they will come northward if all is quiet in South America. Then the battleship squadron will go on to San Francisco and perhaps across the Pacific to Japan."

There was silence for a moment as Topham ceased. Then the President turned to Rutile. "Well, Mr. Rutile," he smiled. "Will that serve?"

"Serve? It will knock the rebellion endways, quiet Japan, and smash the Kaiser's plot. And all without firing a shot. Oh! By *Jove!*" Rutile paused; his feelings were too deep for words.

"Glad you approve," smiled the President. "I understand that Germany's plans depend wholly on the preliminary success of the Brazilian rebellion. If the dispatch of the fleet crushes the rebellion, as I feel assured it will, it ends the whole conspiracy. Further, Mr. Topham, I cabled your report on the San Francisco riot to the Japanese Government last night. A reply has just come stating that the Japanese ambassador here will be recalled and another sent in his place. The inference is that they consider that he was behind the Countess del Ouro Preto in her plot, and wish to disavow it. I don't believe he was, but its about the only thing Japan could do to save her face. Meanwhile, until the new ambassador arrives all claims against the United States will be dropped. This, of course, is confidential. I may add, though— you will see the news in the afternoon papers—that the governor and the leaders of the California legislature are going to be more conciliatory, and avoid giving needless offense to Japan. Also the mayor of San Francisco has promised to prevent any more anti-Japanese riots. So I think everything is about straightened out."

Lillian had been listening with wide-open eyes. For a wonder she had held her tongue. But now she burst out.

"Goody! Goody!" she cried. "Oh! Mr. President, you're just splendid. I can tell you so if these men can't. I'm going to cast my first vote for you when we get women's suffrage, even if it isn't for fifty years!"

The President smiled. "Thank you!" he cried. "I'm sure you won't forget." "Now, gentlemen," he turned back to the two men. "I'm not going to thank you for what you have done. You have done your duty, neither more nor less. For the same reason I'm not going to reward you. But I am going to tell you that I am delighted to know of two—no, three—people who are clever and as capable and as courageous as yourselves. And I'll add that I am going to use you all to the extent of your abilities—not as a reward but simply because you are too capable not to be used. I guess we can find a post as minister somewhere for you, Mr. Rutile. Please consult with the Secretary of State about it. Now, Mr. Topham—"

But Miss Byrd interrupted. "Place aux dames, Mr. President," she cried. "What do I get?"

"What do you want, Miss Byrd?"

"I want three months leave for Mr. Rutile. You see he wants to get married and he's too bashful to tell you."

The President's eyes twinkled. "Oh! Ho! So that's it, is it, Mr. Rutile?" he asked.

Rutile blushed. "Yes! That's it, Mr. President," he admitted.

"Journalism will lose an ornament, but diplomacy will gain one. Mr. Rutile shall have his vacation by all means, Miss Byrd." "Now, Mr. Topham, I have some news for you. It—or rather she—is waiting in the next room. The Countess del Ouro Preto came to see me this morning. She had read the news about the fleet in the papers and knew the game was up. She came to confess, and to tell me a secret or two about herself. Ahem! You have my permission to go, Mr. Topham! Through the right door yonder. Yes! That's it! Good-morning, Mr. Topham."

THE END

Milton Keynes UK
Ingram Content Group UK Ltd.
UKHW030838021124
450589UK00006B/692

9 789362 926289